Re-Situating Utopia

International Legal Theory and Practice

Volumes published in this Brill Research Perspectives title are listed at *brill.com/rplt*

Re-Situating Utopia

By

Matthew Nicholson

BRILL

LEIDEN | BOSTON

This paperback book edition is simultaneously published as issue 1.4 2018, of *International Legal Theory and Practice*, DOI:10.1163/24522058-01030004.

Library of Congress Control Number: 2019951133

Typeface for the Latin, Greek, and Cyrillic scripts: "Brill". See and download: brill.com/brill-typeface.

ISBN 978-90-04-40119-8 (paperback)
ISBN 978-90-04-40120-4 (e-book)

This book is printed on acid-free paper and produced in a sustainable manner.

Contents

Re-Situating Utopia

Matthew Nicholson
Durham University, Durham Law School
matthew.c.nicholson@durham.ac.uk

Abstract

This article considers utopian international legal thought. It makes three interconnected arguments. First, it argues that international law and international legal theory are dominated by a 'blueprint' utopianism that presents international law as the means of achieving a better global future. Second, it argues that such blueprintism makes international law into what philosopher Louis Marin describes as a "degenerate utopia" – a fantastical means of trapping thought and practice within contemporary social and political conditions, blocking any possibility that those conditions might be transcended. Third, it argues for an iconoclastic international legal utopianism – Utopia not as a 'blueprint' for a better future, operating within the confines of existing social and political reality, but as a means of seeking to negate and exit from that reality – as the only way to maintain the idea that international law offers a path towards a truly better future.

Keywords

utopianism – international legal theory – iconoclasm – law and literature – law and philosophy – climate change

Acknowledgements

Thank you to Aoife O'Donoghue and Ruth Houghton for conversations about utopia and everything else, to Kathryn McNeilly for engaging with an early draft, and to Eleni Frantziou for helpful conversations and for commenting on an early draft. Thank you to the organisers of and participants in the

 | DOI:10.1163/9789004401204_002

Inaugural Edinburgh-Glasgow International Law Workshop (Edinburgh, April 2019) – particular thanks to Michelle Burgis-Kasthala for her helpful thoughts as discussant, to Christian Tams for chairing the panel, to Nehal Bhuta for organisation, and to Gerry Simpson for engaging with the argument. Thank you to Richard Joyce, Rose Parfitt and Andrew Benjamin for inviting me to participate in a workshop on authoritarianism (Prato, April 2019) and to participants in that workshop for engaging so helpfully with the ideas. The thoughts presented here have evolved out of PhD research (2009 to 2012) at UCL under the supervision of Catherine Redgwell and Ralph Wilde. I thank Ralph and Catherine for their encouragement and commitment, and UCL's Graduate School for financial support of my doctoral work. My thinking developed further during my time at Southampton Law School (2012–2016), helped along by the good humour of colleagues – particular thanks to David Gurnham, Hazel Biggs and Leonora Onaran for their interest in and support of my work. At Durham Law School I have been fortunate to develop my thinking in conversation with William Lucy, Robert Schütze, Roger Masterman, Shaun Pattinson, Se-shauna Wheatle, Benedict Douglas, Anashri Pillay, Annika Jones, Henry Jones, and Gleider Hernández (now at KU Leuven) and I thank them all. Thank you, most of all, to Gemma and Heather for shining light in darkness. All errors and inadequacies are my fault.

Introduction: Blueprints and Iconoclasm

In this article I propose a re-situation of utopia in international legal thinking, a shift in the way that international legal thinking conceptualises utopia. Attempts to use international law to realise an actual utopia – the notion that "utopia can perhaps finally become incarnate" through "[a] new New International Economic Order,"[1] for example – are, I suggest, misconceived.[2] Such "blueprint" utopianism dominates contemporary international law,[3]

1 Emmanuelle Jouannet, "How to Depart from the Existing Dire Condition of Development" in Antonio Cassese (ed.), *Realizing Utopia: The Future of International Law* (Oxford University Press, 2012) 392, 393.

2 See, for example, Antonio Cassese (ed.), *Realizing Utopia: The Future of International Law* (Oxford University Press, 2012).

3 On 'blueprint' utopianism see Russell Jacoby, *Picture Imperfect: Utopian Thought for an Anti-Utopian Age* (Columbia University Press, 2005), xiv, commenting on the 'blueprint' utopian literature of, for example, Thomas More and Edward Bellamy: "The blueprint utopians map out the future in inches and minutes. From the eating arrangements to the subject of conversation the blueprinters – by far the largest group of utopians – gave precise instructions."

producing a formal, mythical international law – a "degenerate utopia"[4] – that sells a dream of itself as *the* path to a better global future.[5] By deflecting attention away from "the [contemporary] concrete historical situation,"[6] from the scale, depth and intractability of contemporary inequalities and injustices, that dream offers false hope.

In place of "blueprint" attempts to realise utopia through international law it is, I argue, important to recognise that

> utopia is somehow negative ... it is most authentic when we cannot imagine it. Its function lies not in helping us to imagine a better future but rather in demonstrating our utter incapacity to imagine such a future ... reveal[ing in the process] the ideological closure of the system in which we are somehow trapped and confined.[7]

Utopianism is not, then, a means of planning a better future; rather, it charts the limits of contemporary thought and practice. This "iconoclastic utopianism" confronts the challenge of finding a way to overcome the contemporary inability to imagine a future radically different from the present.[8]

The re-situation or shift in international legal thinking I am proposing involves a move from an idea of utopia as a future place planned out in international legal blueprints, to an idea of utopia as a marker of the sense in which international law is "trapped and confined" within contemporary reality.

4 "Degenerate utopia" – Louis Marin (Robert A. Vollrath tr.), *Utopics: Spatial Play* (Humanities Press, 1984), 239: "A degenerate utopia is ideology changed into the form of myth ... Myth is a narrative that resolves formally a fundamental social contradiction."

5 Walter Benjamin (Howard Eiland and Kevin McLaughlin tr.), *The Arcades Project* (Belknap Press of Harvard University Press, 2002), 4, (quoting Jules Michelet): "'Each epoch dreams the one to follow.'" Susan Buck Morss, *The Dialectics of Seeing: Walter Benjamin and the Arcades Project* (MIT Press, 1991), 120: "dream symbols are the fetishized desires that advertise commodities."

6 Benjamin, *Arcades* (n. 5) 391 (K 2,3).

7 Fredric Jameson, "The Politics of Utopia" (2004) 25 *New Left Review* 35, 46.

8 Jacoby (n. 3) xvii–xviii: "[T]he iconoclastic utopians ... [were] resistan[t] to representing the future. They not only obeyed the taboo on graven images, they teetered on the edge of silence about what could be. If the future defied representation, however, it did not defy hope. The iconoclastic utopians were utopians against the current. They did not surrender to the drumbeat of everyday emergencies. Nor did they paint utopia in glowing colors." See also Jacoby, ibid. 85: "The Jewish tradition gave rise to what might be called an iconoclastic utopianism – an anti-utopian utopianism that resisted blueprints. This iconoclastic utopianism was 'anti-utopian' to the extent that it refused to map out the future; it was utopian in its commitment to a very different future of harmony and happiness. The iconoclastic utopians inclined toward the future, but unlike the blueprint utopians, they abstained from depicting it."

The first part of this article outlines iconoclastic utopianism in more detail. The second part – 'Blueprints' – argues that international law maintains an image of itself as a means of planning utopia, a "blueprint" or set of "blueprints" for a better future. I critique the variant forms of this blueprint perspective, focussing on Antonio Cassese's realistic utopianism,[9] Martti Koskenniemi's concern with utopia, particularly in his seminal *From Apology to Utopia*,[10] Philip Allott's utopian effort to "re-imagine the human world by proposing a new ideal of international society,"[11] and Samuel Moyn's work on utopianism and human rights.[12] Cassese, Koskenniemi, Allott and Moyn are the most significant theorists of utopianism in the international legal literature, hence the analysis of their work that follows.

I argue that contemporary international law serves to "represent ... the imaginary relationship individuals maintain with their real conditions of existence,"[13] "a stage for ideological representation,"[14] a "[m]yth ... that resolves [but only] formally [the] ... fundamental social contradiction[s]" of life on earth.[15] Characterising international law's blueprint utopianism in these terms – that is, in terms of ideology, myth and formality – the third part of this article depicts international law as a "degenerate utopia," a term borrowed from philosopher Louis Marin's 1982 analysis of Disneyland (California).[16] Connecting international law's contemporary situation with Marin's Disneyland analysis, I argue that international law's representation of itself as a path to a better future blocks awareness of the sense in which it is now both impossible and essential to imagine a genuine future – a future that does not simply reproduce the present.

In opposition to blueprintism and international law's degenerate utopianism the fourth and final part of the article makes the case for iconoclastic international legal utopianism. Iconoclastic utopianism is, then, the beginning and the end of my argument, the destination I seek to achieve and the

9 See Antonio Cassese, "Introduction" in Antonio Cassese (ed.), *Realizing Utopia: The Future of International Law* (Oxford University Press, 2012) xvii.

10 Martti Koskenniemi, *From Apology to Utopia: The Structure of International Legal Argument – Reissue with New Epilogue* (Cambridge University Press, 2005, first published – without epilogue – in 1989).

11 Philip Allott, *Eunomia: New Order for a New World* (Oxford University Press, 2001 (paperback edition, first published in 1990)) xxvi.

12 See Samuel Moyn, *The Last Utopia: Human Rights in History* (Belknap Press of Harvard University Press, 2010), and part 2(4) below.

13 Marin, *Utopics* (n. 4) 239.

14 Ibid.

15 Ibid.

16 Ibid.

foundation for my critique. It makes sense, then, to start by considering iconoclastic utopianism in more detail.

Part 1: Iconoclastic Utopianism, or "Exiting the Series"

Writing about utopianism and climate change, science fiction author Kim Stanley Robinson notes the impossibility of "[i]magining a positive history that gets us to a better state" whilst insisting on the importance of utopianism in "a significantly damaged biosphere."[17] For Robinson "utopia has gone from being a somewhat minor literary problem to a necessary survival strategy."[18] In the face of something so all-encompassing as climate change utopia becomes a "game of pure contradiction."[19] The impossible and the essential become unachievable yet complementary sides of a utopian process that seeks to "neutral[ise]" what is by offering "the signal for exiting the series" – the system, the international legal order – and "entering into a modifiable destiny."[20]

Utopia as no-place (*Ou-topia*) becomes the only *Eutopia* the only (available) good place.[21] The 'no-place / good place' dialectic expresses the sense in which "[w]e acknowledge this [utopian] place, rather than have knowledge of it [because] [t]he [utopian] 'position' is ... unable to be occupied as such."[22] To think utopia and live with(in) climate change is to pursue the impossible optimistically, accepting the 'no place' impossibility of a life beyond "a significantly damaged biosphere" whilst,[23] at the same time, acknowledging the 'good' of

17 Kim Stanley Robinson, 'Remarks on Utopia in the Age of Climate Change' (2016) 27 *Utopian Studies* 2, 9.

18 Ibid.

19 Marin, *Utopics* (n. 4) xxii.

20 Ibid. xix: "The neutral could be the name given to the signal for exiting the series and for entering into a modifiable destiny, in Bloch's words. The neutral is the *threshold* limiting the inner and the outer, the place where exit and enter reverse and are fixed in this reversal; it is the name for all limits, provided by the thought of the limit: contradiction itself" (emphasis in original). See also Miguel Abensour, "Persistent Utopia" (2008) 15 *Constellations* 406, 409: "Utopia would ... be the exit, the escape of Being, not as Being, but only insofar as Being has become and in unfinished in its becoming. It is this non-achievement of Being, in its gap in relation to essence, that the persistence of utopia resides, the engine of enigmatic rebirth that all the world's conservatives try to conceal by invoking an eternal utopia."

21 Abensour (n. 20) 406: "Utopia is thus a playful name, fruit of [Thomas] More's epigrammatic genius, that permanently oscillates between *eu* and *ou*, between the place where everything is good, the place of bliss (*Eutopia*), and the place of nowhere (*Ou-topia*)."

22 Marin, *Utopics* (n. 4) xix.

23 "A significantly damaged biosphere" – see Robinson quotation at n. 17.

that life and the need to work for it: "utopia as a form is not the representation of radical alternatives; it is rather simply the imperative to imagine them."[24] Iconoclastic utopianism seeks to negate contemporary life (including contemporary international law), approaching the essentially negative question of why a better future has not been and is not in the process of being realised as the positive foundation for radical changes in contemporary thought and action.[25]

For sociologist Zygmunt Bauman contemporary ideas of happiness involve the reproduction of the present in place of any attempt to build a genuine future: "happiness means now a different today rather than a more felicitous tomorrow, as it did in the past."[26] The permanence of commodified existence makes fundamental social change unimaginable:

> The globe is full. There are no as yet undiscovered places left and no place where one could hide from the order (or for that matter disorder) ruling (or for that matter misruling) in places already known and mapped, criss-crossed by beaten tracks, administered and managed. In this world, there is no more 'outside.'[27]

If everything and everywhere is inter-connected there can be no no-place:

> 'Utopia' – in its original meaning of a place that does not exist – has become, within the logic of the globalized world, a contradiction in terms. The 'nowhere' (the 'forever nowhere', the 'thus-far-nowhere', and the 'nowhere-as-yet' alike) is no more a place.[28]

To suggest otherwise *via* utopian blueprints dilutes the goodness or *Eu*topia of Utopia because of a failure to recognise the limits that contemporary social, political and economic conditions place on imagination and creativity. Contemporary utopianism must recognise that any blueprint for the future

---

24 Fredric Jameson, "'If I Can Find One Good City I Will Spare the Man': Realism and Utopia in Kim Stanley Robinson's *Mars* Trilogy" in Fredric Jameson, *Archaeologies of the Future: The Desire Called Utopia and Other Science Fictions* (Verso, 2007) 393, 416.

25 See Jameson, "The Politics of Utopia" (n. 7) 46: "utopianism involves a certain distance from the political institutions which encourages an endless play of fantasy around their possible reconstructions and restructurations."

26 Zygmunt Bauman, "Utopia with No Topos" (2003) 16(1) *History of the Human Sciences* 23, 24 (original in italics), and see 23: "Happiness and more happiness are desired now as they used to be in bygone times of utopia-writing."

27 Ibid. 22.

28 Ibid.

formed in contemporary commodified, consumerist globalised conditions will be determined by those conditions, by "our own absolute limits."[29]

Iconoclastic utopianism, in opposition to blueprint utopianism, emphasises the importance of contemporary conditions through a particular understanding of time, and its division into past, present and future. In *The Political Unconscious* cultural and literary theorist Fredric Jameson advocates a method of literary analysis that "foreground[s] the interpretive categories or codes through which we read and receive the text in question."[30] Jameson proposes this method in opposition to a focus on the internal aspects or "structures of a given cultural text."[31] For Jameson texts are to be understood in their cultural (including social and political) context, rather than in their own right or on their own terms. Expanding on this theme in his later work, Jameson argues that an understanding of the contemporary condition – the contemporary 'cultural logic' – is the foundation for analysis of contemporary conditions and any attempt to change them: "'We have to name the system.'"[32] As parts of "the system," time and history are culturally conditioned categories or concepts: 'the past', 'the present' and 'the future' do not mean the same thing to all people, in all places, at all times. Those terms are to be understood by reference to the prevailing cultural conditions of any particular time or moment.

Jameson attempts to capture prevailing, contemporary cultural conditions under the label 'postmodernism', a famously contested term that he defines as "the consumption of sheer commodification as a process."[33] Time and history are, on Jameson's analysis, excluded or marginalised within postmodernism because of "historical deafness."[34] The resulting "crisis in historicity" originates in the cultural supremacy of consumption and commodification.[35] That

29 Jameson, "Progress Versus Utopia, Or Can We Imagine the Future?" in Fredric Jameson, *Archaeologies of the Future: The Desire Called Utopia and Other Science Fictions* (Verso, 2007) 281, 288–289: "[Science fiction's] deepest vocation is over and over again to demonstrate and to dramatize our incapacity to imagine the future, to body forth, through apparently full representations which prove on closer inspection to be structurally and constitutively impoverished, the atrophy in our time of what Marcuse has called the *utopian imagination*, the imagination of otherness and radical difference; to succeed by failure, to serve as unwitting and even unwilling vehicles for a meditation, which, setting forth into the unknown, finds itself irrevocably mired in the all-too-familiar, and thereby becomes unexpectedly transformed into a contemplation of our own absolute limits" (emphasis in original).

30 Fredric Jameson, *The Political Unconscious: Narrative as a socially symbolic act* (Routledge, 1983) ix.

31 Ibid.

32 Fredric Jameson, *Postmodernism, or The Cultural Logic of Late Capitalism* (Verso, 1991) 418.

33 Ibid. x.

34 Ibid. xi.

35 Ibid. 25.

crisis manifests itself in "an increasingly absolute self-reproduction,"[36] creating "a new and original historical situation in which we are condemned to seek History by way of our own pop images and simulacra of that history, which itself remains forever out of reach."[37] Engagement with the past functions at the level of "pastiche" – "the imitation of a peculiar or unique, idiosyncratic style, the wearing of a linguistic mask, speech in a dead language"[38] – granting access to "a stereotypical past."[39] Rigorous inquiry into the minutiae of what was is sacrificed in pursuit of aesthetic appeal to present day audiences, because history as commodity will only sell if it "trace[s] *our* [present-day] mental images of [the] … past."[40] As a consequence, "the past is dead, transformed into a packet of well-worn and thumbed glossy images."[41]

Within the commodified conditions of the postmodern, the systemic structure of the present is as inaccessible or invisible as the past. The supremacy of aesthetics and the requirement for "absolute self-reproduction" means that "we seem increasingly incapable of fashioning representations of our own current experience."[42] Jameson proposes science-fiction ('SF') literature as the best available means of representing the present to ourselves:

> [T]he apparent realism, of representationality, of SF has concealed another, far more complex temporal structure: not to give us "images" of the future – whatever such images might mean for a reader who will necessarily predecease their "materialization" – but rather to defamiliarize and restructure our experience of our own present, and to do so in specific ways distinct from all other forms of defamilarization … [Marcel] Proust was only the most monumental "high" literary expression of this discovery: that the present – in this society, and in the physical and psychic dissociation of the human subjects who inhabit it – is inaccessible directly, is numb, habituated, empty of affect. Elaborate strategies of

36 Ibid. 65

37 Ibid. 25.

38 Ibid. 17.

39 Ibid. 21.

40 Ibid. 25 (emphasis ('*our*') added): "[The] historical novel can no longer set out to represent the historical past; it can only 'represent' our ideas and stereotypes about that past (which thereby at one becomes 'pop history'). Cultural production is thereby driven back inside a mental space which is no longer that of the old monadic subject but rather that of some degraded collective 'objective spirit': it can no longer gaze directly on some putative real world, at some reconstruction of a past history which was once itself a present; rather, as in Plato's cave, it must trace our mental images of that past upon its confining walls."

41 Jameson, "Progress Versus Utopia" (n. 29) 287.

42 Jameson, *Postmodernism* (n. 32) 21.

> indirection are therefore necessary if we are somehow to break through our monadic insulation and to "experience," for some first and real time, this "present," which is after all all we have.[43]

If postmodern conditions insulate us from the fundamental nature or systematicity of present reality, they equally make a genuine future – a future fundamentally different from present reality – unimaginable: "the future ... may still be alive in some small heroic collectivities on the Earth's surface ... [but] is for [most of] us either irrelevant or unthinkable."[44] This supposedly "eternal present" is a utopia[45] – a totalising vision of what exists as *all* there is, "as if the world itself can be the object of a final land survey,"[46] an "exactly closed totality rigorously coded by all the constraints and obligations of the law binding and closing a place with insuperable frontiers that would guarantee its harmonious functioning."[47] In what follows I will argue that international legal utopianism has, to date, chosen to accept the limits of contemporary postmodern conditions, drafting blueprints whose content is (more or less consciously) determined by those conditions. I argue that international legal utopianism should chose the other option, embracing the impossible, iconoclastic "imperative" of imagining "radical alternatives" to contemporary reality.[48]

Costas Douzinas, perhaps the only legal scholar to embrace iconoclastic utopianism, notes the impossibility of a genuine future, and of blueprints that seek to plan it from within present conditions:

> We cannot stop criticising the present and we cannot do that without adopting the position of the future; but, similarly, we can never remove ourselves sufficiently from our here and now to adopt the redemptive position. Utopian hope is necessary and impossible; a general utopian plan, if imposed on people, risks becoming a blueprint for worse oppression and domination.[49]

---

43 Jameson, "Progress Versus Utopia" (n. 29) 286–287.

44 Ibid. 287–288.

45 "Eternal present" – Fredric Jameson, *The Antinomies of Realism* (Verso, 2013) 24, 26, 28, 39–41.

46 Louis Marin, "Frontiers of Utopia: Past and Present" (1993) 19(3) *Critical Inquiry* 397, 399.

47 Ibid. 403–404.

48 See Jameson quotation at n. 24.

49 Costas Douzinas, "Human Rights and Postmodern Utopia" (2000) 11 *Law and Critique* 219, 238.

The internal logic of a contemporary present that posits its own permanence makes the future "irrelevant or unthinkable."[50] The permanent and total has no concept of what lies beyond it because there is no 'beyond'. With the fall of communism, the end of the Cold War, and the triumph of "free" markets history has (apparently) ended. Society, politics and human affairs have reached their end state and this, now, is utopia, is all there is.[51] As scholar of utopian thought Ruth Levitas, writing in 2000, puts it: "[C]apitalism is widely held to be the only game in town ... [and] [p]ost-1989, it might be said that we live, in an almost biblical sense, after the fall, but with no hope of redemption."[52]

Douzinas, writing in 2000, suggests that in postmodern conditions "utopia can be defined as the remembrance of the future."[53] Louis Marin, writing in 1993, anticipates that perspective:

> At the end of a millennium ... when singing out loud the end of the ideologies and the end of frontiers seems to be accomplished in a universal totality – when, in recent debates, there is confusedly and loudly forecast ... the end of history ... as the universal mode of high-tech democratic hyperliberalism ... – precisely at this moment it is worthwhile to recall the fiction of an island appearing at the dawn of a period for which the present time would be the twilight.[54]

Echoing Bauman's phrase – "happiness means now a different today rather than a more felicitous tomorrow, as it did in the past"[55] – in these anti-utopian times what passes for utopianism is, Levitas maintains, often "pragmatic, limited reformism ... essentially anti-utopian in its rejection of radical utopian otherness or fundamental social transformation."[56]

---

50 "Irrelevant or unthinkable" – see Jameson quotation at n. 44.

51 Douzinas, (n. 49) 236: "The concept of utopia was dealt the first debilitating blow in the fifties and sixties when the Soviet gulags and mental asylums became widely known. It was deleted from the political dictionary with the collapse of communism. In this anti-utopian climate, Francis Fukuyama earned world-wide fame when he stated that 'today, we have trouble imagining a world that is radically better than our own, or a future that is not *essentially* democratic and capitalist ... We cannot picture to ourselves a world that is essentially different from the present one, and at the same time better'" (emphasis in original).

52 Ruth Levitas, "For Utopia: The (Limits of the) Utopian Function in Late Capitalist Society" (2000) 3(2–3) *Critical Review of International Social and Political Philosophy* 25, 31.

53 Douzinas (n. 49) 226.

54 Marin, "Frontiers" (n. 46) 411–412.

55 See Bauman quotation at n. 26.

56 Levitas (n. 52) 31.

I want to suggest that pragmatic, realist anti-utopianism dominates international legal thought in the form of various blueprints for a "different today." My argument is that international legal thought and scholarship must re-situate its understanding of utopianism by replacing blueprintism with iconoclasm because if that does not happen international law, as a "degenerate utopia" (see the third part of this article) – a utopia that merely reforms, repackages and re-presents what is – will not even begin to be capable of grappling with the existential threat of climate change. Incapacity to engage with climate change is not, of course, the only basis on which international legal blueprintism can be critiqued and a more wide-ranging critique will be developed in what follows. But it is, as Kim Stanley Robinson suggests,[57] the most compelling and decisive because it demonstrates the absolute, existential imperative of a future that does not continue to reproduce the present.

If the contemporary, postmodern present is an order or system built on the supposed permanence of a commodified, consumerist reality, subordinating everything to processes of commodification and consumption and manifesting a "totalitarian desire for power" over past, present and future realities,[58] utopia(nism) is a way of insisting on "the limits of any state, any institution."[59] For Louis Marin Utopia is "a displaced map displacing all maps and really finding none,"[60] a "'sign of the authentic end [that] opens into emptiness ... [that] does not announce a new series ... [but] leads out of the series ... giv[ing] the signal that we are coming out of the series ... that we are entering into the possible, the unfated ... [or] at least into a fate that can be modified.'"[61] Like Marin, critical theorist Theodor Adorno promotes resistance to any order or condition: "An order that shuts itself up in its own meaning will shut itself away from the possibility above order."[62] I argue that the international legal order needs to discover and be open to "the possibility above" it. Rather than seeking to contain or repel challenges to its orderliness by insisting on its unity, coherence, and systematicity, challenges to international law's integrity need to be seen as moments of utopian possibility, chances for international law to embrace the possibility of a genuine future. Political philosopher Miguel Abensour captures something of this in his reflections on catastrophe and utopia:

57 See text at n. 17 and n. 18.

58 Marin, "Frontiers" (n. 46) 420.

59 Ibid.

60 Ibid. 417.

61 Ibid. 420 (quoting Ernst Bloch).

62 Theodor W. Adorno, *Negative Dialectics* (Continuum, 2007 [1966]) 397.

> [F]rom catastrophe ... arises a new utopian summation, the "never again" that immediately expresses, beyond the banality of the formulation, the exigency of utopia, as if catastrophe has *a contrario* revealed the necessity of utopia ... The time of history is not homogeneous, empty material; it bears forever inscribed in it, despite forgetting, the wounds of the past, the trace of rupture.[63]

"[R]upture" expresses the utopian possibility of each event or moment, its capacity to negate what is and open "order" up to "the possibility above" it. Cultural and literary critic Walter Benjamin recognises the potential of the singular moment as a break, rejecting the idea of history as a process of "establishing a causal nexus" – an order, a pattern – "among various moments of history" and the notion of a "homogeneous, empty time."[64] He prefers "a conception of the present as now-time shot through with the splinters of messianic time" and the notion that "every second was the small gateway in time through which the Messiah might enter."[65] In similar terms, Abensour argues that "once we have drunk from the cup of utopian displacement, any enclosure, any installation in a place would become inconceivable."[66] Utopia, for Abensour, is defined by its "persistence," "its very fluidity and plasticity," its pursuit of "ephemeral but nevertheless interminable lines of flight that open breaches."[67]

In promoting an iconoclastic international legal utopianism, in place of the "blueprint" utopianism that I suggest currently dominates international legal thinking, I am arguing that Utopia, *as* a negative no-place (*Ou-topia*), *is* international law's *Eutopia* (good place). The dialectical relationship between non-existence and good-ness, expressed in ideas of impossibility, imperative, negation, and neutralisation outlined above, offers "ephemeral ... interminable lines of flight" that international legal thought should, I suggest, follow.

63 Abensour (n. 20) 419.

64 Walter Benjamin, "On the Concept of History" in Walter Benjamin (Howard Eiland and Michael W. Jennings eds.), *Selected Writings: Volume 4 1938–1940* (Belknap Press of Harvard University Press, 2006) 389, 397.

65 Ibid.

66 Abensour (n. 20) 418.

67 Ibid.

Part 2: Blueprints

1 *Being "Within": Antonio Cassese, Martti Koskenniemi and the Utopian Possibility of International Law*

In the introduction to *Realizing Utopia*, his 2012 edited collection, Antonio Cassese considers three attitudes outlined by dystopian author Aldous Huxley.[68] First, the attitude of "the *Technicians*, who ... are inclined 'to accept too complacently the main framework of the structure whose details they are trying to improve'"; next, the attitude of "the *Utopians*, who 'are much too preoccupied with what ought to be to pay any serious attention to what is'"; and finally, the attitude of "the *Judicious Reformers*" who, according to Cassese, "[are] ... alert to the present ... suggest[ing] realistic and viable avenues in order to avoid, at least to some extent, those pitfalls encountered when trying to build a better path."[69] Cassese prefers the outlook of the judicious reformer, presenting his "realistic utopia[nism]" as "miles away from the traditional conception of utopia,"[70] and preferring "new avenues for improving the major deficiencies of the current society of states" to utopian ideals of "comity, friendship, and cooperation."[71] Presented in these terms, Cassese's project is more concerned with reform than Utopia.

Various "avenues" are pursued in the book's forty-seven chapters – explorations of 'global community' such as Philip Alston's proposals for UN reform or Anne Peters review of international legal constitutionalism,[72] or normative reforms such as Nils Melzer's proposal to "[bolster] the protection of civilians in armed conflict."[73] Walking down these "avenues" the judicious reformer "moves on the solid ground of 'critical positivism',"[74] "engaging ... in imaginative thinking" whilst "refrain[ing] from chasing unattainable dreams."[75]

---

68 See Aldous Huxley, *Brave New World* (Chatto & Windus, 1932).

69 Cassese, "Introduction" (n. 9) xvii–xviii (quoting Huxley).

70 Ibid. xviii and xxi.

71 Ibid. xxi.

72 Philip Alston, "The United Nations: No Hope for Reform?" in Antonio Cassese (ed.), *Realizing Utopia: The Future of International Law* (Oxford University Press, 2012) 38; Anne Peters, "Are we Moving towards Constitutionalization of the World Community?" in Antonio Cassese (ed.), *Realizing Utopia: The Future of International Law* (Oxford University Press, 2012) 118.

73 Nils Melzer, "Bolstering the Protection of Civilians in Armed Conflict" in Antonio Cassese (ed.), *Realizing Utopia: The Future of International Law* (Oxford University Press, 2012) 508.

74 Cassese, "Introduction" (n. 9) xvii.

75 Ibid., xxi, xxii.

In this determinedly realistic sense Cassese has a "belief in law as a means to realize Utopia,"[76] and he seems to share that belief with his contributors. Martti Koskenniemi, for example, suggests that as a "realistic utopia ... that begin[s] with the critique of present institutions" international law sustains the possibility of "invit[ing] the widest possible participation by everyone, but especially those in the global South,"[77] encouraging a Kantian utopianism of "critique and contestation" that "start[s] from here and now ... judg[ing] present institutions in view of the maximization of freedom tomorrow."[78] Most of Cassese's contributors prefer a more practical-doctrinal concept of utopia, however, focussing on institutional or normative reforms – consider Bardo Fassbender's proposal for a Security Council that "attaches more importance to collective goods and interests of all peoples inhabiting the earth than to the individual goods and interests of the states represented in the Council,"[79] or Jérome de Hemptinne's "Blueprint for Action" on "The Future of International Criminal Justice."[80] Anxieties about realism – about connections with and plausibility in the context of what is – mean that this is not a project in search of Utopia but a limited "blueprint" for a reformed legal future.

Cassese is not the first international lawyer to attempt a balancing act between Utopia and realism. Martti Koskenniemi's *From Apology to Utopia* charts the opposition between the "concrete" reality of an international law made by states and a strongly "normative" international law built on conceptions of 'the good':[81]

---

76 Isabel Feichtner, "Realizing Utopia through the Practice of International Law" (2012) 23 *European Journal of International Law* 1143, 1144.

77 Martti Koskenniemi, "Utopia as Critique" in Antonio Cassese (ed.), *Realizing Utopia: The Future of International Law* (Oxford University Press, 2012) 3, 12.

78 Ibid., 13, 12.

79 Bardo Fassbender, "The Security Council: Progress is Possible but Unlikely" in Antonio Cassese (ed.), *Realizing Utopia: The Future of International Law* (Oxford University Press, 2012) 52, 58.

80 Jérome de Hemptinne, "The Future of International Criminal Justice: A Blueprint for Action" in Antonio Cassese (ed.), *Realizing Utopia: The Future of International Law* (Oxford University Press, 2012) 585.

81 Koskenniemi, *From Apology* (n. 10) 58: "The requirement of concreteness related to the need to verify the law's content not against some political principles but by reference to the concrete behaviour, will and interest of States. The requirement of normativity related to the capacity of the law to be opposable to State policy ... A doctrine with much concreteness seemed to lose its normative nature and end up in descriptive apology. A truly normative doctrine created a gap between itself and State practice in a manner which made doubtful the objectivity of the method of verifying its norms. It ended up in undemonstrable utopias." I develop a more comprehensive analysis of Koskenniemi's oeuvre – the analysis here being limited to Koskenniemi's engagement with utopia – in

> A law which would lack distance from State behaviour will or interest would amount to a non-normative apology, a mere sociological description. A law which would base itself on principles which are unrelated to State behaviour, will or interest would seem utopian, incapable of demonstrating its own content in any reliable way.[82]

Koskenniemi offers no solution to the oscillation between concreteness (reality) and normativity (utopia) because, on his analysis, international law is defined by "the dynamics of [this] contradiction."[83] Whilst Koskenniemi's approach identifies qualifiedly utopian possibilities within the existing international legal structure, Cassese advocates realistically utopian reforms to that structure. Both define their utopianism by reference to the realities of contemporary international law, tacitly rejecting approaches that would pursue a non-existent no-place (*Ou-topia*) or an unqualifiedly good place (*Eutopia*).

Opportunities for the kind of "critique and contestation" that Koskenniemi advocates are to be found in gaps or indeterminacies in international legal discourse.[84] International legal indeterminacy originates in the opposition between concreteness and normativity,[85] in the possibility of basing legal arguments on either normative goals or the concretely expressed will of states.[86] The inherent nature of that indeterminacy – the impossibility of resolving it by preferring either normativity or concreteness – leads Koskenniemi to conclude that "law is incapable of providing convincing justifications to the solution of normative problems."[87] This indeterminacy means that international lawyers have to make choices that are not dictated by the law's content or structure.[88] In making such choices international lawyers practice hegemony. Hegemony is

---

Matthew Nicholson, "Psychoanalyzing International Law(yers)" (2017) 18(3) *German Law Journal* 441.

82 Koskenniemi, *From Apology* (n. 10) 17.

83 Ibid. 58. See also ibid. 65: "[D]octrine is forced to maintain itself *in constant movement from emphasizing concreteness to emphasizing normativity and vice-versa* without being able to establish itself permanently in either position" (emphasis in original).

84 "Critique and contestation" – see Koskenniemi quotation at n. 78.

85 See Koskenniemi, *From Apology* (n. 10) 28–58 and 590–596 on indeterminacy.

86 Ibid. 63: "International legal discourse is incoherent as it incorporates *contradictory assumptions* about what it is to argue objectively about norms. This gives rise to conflicting legal arguments and the inability to prefer any of them" (emphasis in original).

87 Ibid. 69.

88 See ibid. 69: "I believe that lawyers should admit that if they wish to achieve justifications, they have to take a stand on political issues without assuming that there exists a privileged rationality which solves such issues for them." See also ibid. 536: "[L]awyers expectations of certainty should be downgraded ... they – as well as States and statesmen – must take seriously the moral-political choices they are faced with when arguing 'within the law'

a particular form of decision-making in circumstances of socio-political incoherence where the supposedly governing texts do not dictate the outcome.[89] The practice of international legal hegemony expresses the "realistic utopia" of "critique and contestation" that Koskenniemi contemplates in his contribution to Cassese's edited collection,[90] reflecting the possibility of achieving limited yet positive change within international law's structure.

Koskenniemi characterises his approach as "more [of] ... a critical standpoint from which to attack any present (functional) architecture for falling short of the ideal of freedom than a constructive platform on which to impose any particular blueprint on the world."[91] Whilst he does not offer a detailed, 'build-to-print' utopian plan, Koskenniemi sketches a utopian blueprint: an image of international law as a frame within which Utopia might be built. That frame consists of formal political equality – "the widest possible participation by everyone, but especially those in the global South";[92] a vague notion of freedom – "judge present institutions in view of the maximization of freedom tomorrow";[93] and an image of extant international law as a Utopia of sorts – a good place / no-place that affords something unavailable in the non-legal, 'real' world:

> In the absence of agreement over, or knowledge of the "true" objectives of political community – that is to say, in an agnostic world – the pure form of international law provides the shared surface – the *only* such surface – on which political adversaries recognize each other as such and pursue their adversity in terms of something shared, instead of seeking to attain full exclusion – "outlawry" – of the other. In this sense, international law's value and its misery lie in its being the fragile surface of political community among social agents – States, other communities, individuals – who

---

and accept the consequence that in some relevant sense the choices are theirs and that they therefore should be responsible for them."

89 See Ernesto Laclau and Chantal Mouffe, *Hegemony and Socialist Strategy: Towards a Radical Democratic Politics* (2nd edition, Verso, 2001). For a detailed exploration of the links between Koskenniemi's and Laclau's and Mouffe's work, and the centrality of hegemony to Koskenniemi's international legal theory, see Nicholson, "Psychoanalyzing" (n. 81).

90 "Critique and contestation" – see Koskenniemi quotation at n. 78.

91 Koskenniemi, "Utopia as Critique" (n. 77) 12.

92 Ibid. (also quoted at n. 77 above).

93 Ibid.

> disagree about their preferences but do this *within* a structure that invites them to argue in terms of an assumed universality.[94]

Cassese and Koskenniemi "[shut international law] up in its own [extant] meaning ... away from the possibilit[ies] above [the extant international legal] order" by focussing on the limited utopian possibilities *within* existing international law.[95] As outlined in the part one, I argue that this is the wrong choice and that it is now vital to investigate the "possibility above [the extant international legal] order."[96] That argument is, of course, not fully developed at this point; that will have to wait until the last part of this article. But in this section I have sought to demonstrate that Cassese and Koskenniemi – perhaps the best known international legal utopians in the literature – quite deliberately fit their utopian ambitions into extant international law, remaining "trapped and confined" within "the system" as a result.[97]

Akbar Rasulov, in perhaps the most recent reflection on international legal utopianism in the literature, prefers investment in the extant international legal system to international legal utopianism.[98] For Rasulov "the single greatest favour one could ever render to the idea of international legal utopianism is to relieve it of any great theoretical duties."[99] Rasulov prefers "study [of] the practical givens of law's social reality" to utopian projects that seek to re-make international law,[100] largely because international law, with its goal of "a single worldwide regime of the rule of law,"[101] is and always has been

94 Martti Koskenniemi, "What is International Law For?" in Malcolm D. Evans (ed.), *International Law* (4th edition, Oxford University Press, 2014) 29, 48 (emphasis – "*only*" – in third line of quotation in original; emphasis – "*within*" – in final line added).

95 Adorno, *Negative Dialectics* (n. 62) 397 (also quoted at n. 62).

96 See text at n. 62 to n. 63.

97 "Trapped and confined" and "the system" – see Jameson quotation at n. 7 above.

98 Akbar Rasulov, "The Utopians" in Jean d'Aspremont and Sahib Singh (eds.), *Concepts for International Law: Contributions to Disciplinary Thought* (Edward Elgar 2019) 879. See ibid. 899: "There is no theoretical value – nor, indeed, should there be any political reason – in continuing any form of investment, discursive or otherwise, in that synthetic abstraction ... the utopian international lawyer as a (purported) disciplinary ideal type. Let the empty chimeras stay where they belong – outside our system of operative analytical categories."

99 Ibid. 898–899.

100 Ibid. 898.

101 Ibid. 897: "[I]f the ultimate hallmark of the utopian approach is that its proponents always tend to go off on a quest for some non-existent unicorn, to grab for the future instead of working for it patiently in the present, to fantasize impotently and to fall ill with longing, then the ultimate question that ought to confront every international lawyer at this point, surely, must be: has there ever been an enterprise that was more utopian – more hubristic,

utopian. Consistent with Cassese's and Koskenniemi's approach Rasulov invests in such utopianism as exists within international law, excluding the "possibility above [the extant international legal] order" that the argument advanced here invests in.[102]

2 *Fragments of a Legal Utopia*

Consistent with Cassese's and Koskenniemi's 'within'-ness, a number of voices argue that there are aspects or fragments of utopia – limited legal blueprints for a slightly improved future – within international law.

Writing in 1985, Alexandre Kiss suggests a certain utopianism in the "common heritage of mankind" regimes in the Antarctic Treaty, the international legal framework governing activities on the moon, and the United Nations Convention on the Law of the Sea's framework governing 'the Area'[103] – 'the Area' being "the seabed and ocean floor and subsoil thereof, beyond the limits of national jurisdiction."[104] The idea that by operation of law the Antarctic, the moon, and 'the Area' are placed beyond exclusionary claims of national ownership certainly has a utopian quality in the context of contemporary processes of commodification and consumption. But Kiss is pessimistic about the prospects of realising this "common heritage" Utopia, noting that enforcement of these normative frameworks cannot be guaranteed given the absence of compulsory jurisdiction over states for international courts.[105]

Richard Falk, in a 1964 article about "the condition of international legal theory in the United States,"[106] recommends "a discouraging realism and a qualified commitment to utopian objectives" in view of the "tragic paradox" that "effective management of violence in world affairs" is a "necessity" whilst

more delusional, a product of greater infantilism and a false sense of confidence – than the *very project of modern international law itself*, with its naïve plans to replace the 'political' with the 'international', to bring into existence a single worldwide regime of the rule of law without creating a corresponding system of enforcement institutions, a global legal order without a world government?" (emphasis in original).

102 See text at n. 62 to n. 63.

103 Alexandre Kiss, "The common heritage of mankind: utopia or reality?" (1985) 40(3) *International Journal* 423; Antarctic Treaty, 402 UNTS 71 (no. 5778), as discussed by Kiss, ibid., at 428; Agreement Governing the Activities of States on the Moon and Other Celestial Bodies, 610 UNTS 305 (no. 8843), as discussed by Kiss, ibid., at 431; United Nations Convention on the Law of the Sea ('UNCLOS'), 1833 UNTS 3 (no. 31363), as discussed by Kiss, ibid., at 431–433.

104 UNCLOS, ibid., Art. 1.

105 Kiss (n. 103) 440.

106 Richard Falk, "The Adequacy of Contemporary Theories of international Law – Gaps in Legal Thinking" (1964) 50(2) *Virginia Law Review* 231, 231.

"achieving management by consensual means" is "impossible."[107] Falk's qualified utopianism informs his assessment of the UN Charter's collective security regime: "[C]ompared to the League [of Nations], the United Nations constitutes a more ambitious attempt to create a visible institutional center for international society competent, if not capable, to restrain recourse to violence by nations."[108] Falk is in search of blueprints, more interested in plans or "techniques for getting from here to there than [in] ... a vision of what it will be like when we get there."[109] Whilst the UN Charter is not a utopian blueprint, there are faint outlines of a better future, "a model ... a helpful guide."[110]

The utopian dimension of the *jus ad bellum* suggested by Falk is widely recognised in the literature. Writing in the pre-Charter days of 1943 Georg Schwarzenberger, for example, notes that perspectives differ as "the emphasis changes from war as the natural state of relations between States to peace as 'a state most highly agreeable to human nature.'"[111] If "[r]eality and utopia often are amalgamated in the picture of the state of nature" then Utopia is one component in "a sociological analysis of international law ... as an ideology, reality and utopia."[112]

Marc Weller, writing in 2018, goes beyond Falk's and Schwarzenberger's cautious utopianism, concluding that "the legal system on the use of force ... is principally utopian in character, both in terms of its substantive rules and its process requirements."[113] For Weller "utopia is not an 'un-place'" because "[t]he League Covenant and its successor, the UN Charter, reflect all the major elements that would ordinarily be characterised as utopian when put forward as a programmatic proposal."[114] Weller goes so far as to suggest that through the law on the use of force "the international legal system has developed beyond Utopia, in ways Sir Thomas More and his successors would have found difficult to imagine, or perhaps even to endorse."[115] All that remains, according to Weller, is for this utopian legal framework to become "fully effective."[116]

---

107 Ibid. 247–248 (parts of the original text are in italics).

108 Ibid. 246.

109 Ibid. 249.

110 Ibid.

111 Georg Schwarzenberger, "Jus Pacis Ac Belli?: Prolegomena to a Sociology of International Law" (1943) 37(3) *American Journal of International Law* 460, 460 (quoting Pufendorf).

112 Ibid. 460, 479.

113 Marc Weller, "The Real Utopia: International Constitutionalism and The Use of Force" in Robert Schütze (ed.), *Globalization and Governance: International Problems, European Solutions* (Cambridge University Press, 2018) 131, 146.

114 Ibid. 137.

115 Ibid. 146.

116 Ibid. 147.

Balancing latent utopian potential with a failure to match that potential in implementation – a familiar theme in much of the international legal analysis considered so far, with the notable exception of Weller – Costas Douzinas laments the "conformism which threatens human rights when they become a tool of states, governments and international organisations."[117] Douzinas maintains some hope for Utopia as "the name for the great power of imagination which finds the future latent in every cultural product … preserv[ing] the kernel of radical enthusiasm in every ideology it criticises."[118]

Some see utopian potential in the concept of a universal jurisdiction, permitting all national courts to try international crimes regardless of the nationality of the accused or connection between the offence and the forum state. Lisa Hajjar welcomes the chaos in inter-state relations that such universal jurisdiction would cause,[119] whilst Fannie Lafontaine describes universal jurisdiction as "the realistic utopia."[120] Darryl Robinson uses Koskenniemi's apology-utopia dialectic to review criticisms of the International Criminal Court.[121] Noting that the court is critiqued for being too close to the whims of states (apology) and for being too detached from the realities of inter-state relations (utopia),[122] Robinson concludes that "the impossibility of the [international criminal law] project need not undermine its necessity."[123]

Across the literature, from Cassese's realism, *via* Koskenniemi's structuralism, to Robinson's reflections on international criminal law, there is a determination to find and invest in extant international law's (limited) Utopia. Philip Allott inverts that approach, rejecting the pursuit of the utopian within existing international law as the first step in re-forming international law and building a global, utopian society.

---

117 Douzinas, (n. 49) 226.

118 Ibid. 224.

119 Lisa Hajjar, "Chaos as Utopia: International Criminal Prosecutions as a Challenge to State Power" (2004) 31 *Studies in Law, Politics and Society* 3, 9, extolling "the political productivity of legal violence to attack impunity by making the powerful vulnerable, and [the] value of chaos made possible by the threat legal violence poses to public officials responsible for gross violations."

120 Fannie Lafontaine, "Universal Jurisdiction – the Realistic Utopia" (2012) 10 *Journal of International Criminal Justice* 1277.

121 Darryl Robinson, "Inescapable Dyads: Why the International Criminal Court Cannot Win" (2015) 28 *Leiden Journal of International Law* 323. On Koskenniemi's apology-utopia dialectic see text at n. 82.

122 Robinson ibid. 325–326.

123 Ibid., 347.

3 *On the Outside: Phillip Allott's Eutopianism*

Philip Allott works from outside extant international law, challenging it to become more than it is or has been.[124] In *Eunomia*, first published in 1990, Allott "seeks to invoke the power of the future to re-imagine the human world by proposing a new ideal of international society, the society of all-humanity, the society of all societies."[125] The law of this meta-society is, on Allott's analysis, "an emerging universal legal system, the legal system of all legal systems,"[126] arising out of post-Cold War processes of globalization and associated changes in the way people think and live.[127]

Allott contrasts "old international law" – "typically the law acknowledged by governments and their advisers and consecrated by the International Court of Justice in The Hague" – with a "new international law ... made in countless international forums, implemented through countless international agencies, interpreted and applied by countless new international courts and tribunals ... re-enacted by national legislatures, implemented by national executive branches of government, [and] enforced in national courts."[128] Reflecting on his experience as a legal adviser in the British Foreign and Commonwealth Office, he critiques the sense in which "[t]he masters of the world of tomorrow are the slaves of yesterday's ideas,"[129] noting that "the international system itself is nothing other than a structure of ideas."[130] "[W]ithdrawing to the cloisters of Cambridge in 1973,"[131] Allott describes his attempt to "understand and then to change the systematic structure of international society" in light of his Foreign Office experience,[132] having resolved "to create a new total view of society and law":[133]

---

124 See Anthony Carty, "Social Theory and the 'Vanishing' of International Law: A Review Article" (1992) 41 *International and Comparative Law Quarterly* 939, 939, commenting on Allott's *Eunomia*: "the discipline [international law] is subsumed under much wider categories ... [Allott] appear[s] to ignore the form-content or procedure-substance distinction in international law"; 940: "Allott presents himself as an *outsider*" (emphasis in original).

125 Allott, *Eunomia* (n. 11) xxvi.

126 Ibid. xxv

127 Ibid. xiii–xxiv.

128 Ibid. xv.

129 Ibid. xlv.

130 Ibid.

131 Ibid.

132 Ibid.

133 Ibid. xlvi.

> [T]he task always a practical one – to form a view which could become the normal content of consciousness of all those involved, closely or distantly, in national government and in international society, eventually replacing the existing theoretical structures completely.[134]

This, then, is ideational blueprint utopianism: a practical project that seeks to change the "consciousness" of all relevant actors. Allott asserts the distinctive law-ness of international law *and* the necessity of its connection with social reality, valuing Hans Kelsen's work because it "grounded legal obligation in the coherence of a closed system of obligation,"[135] whilst praising Myres McDougal's effort to "integrate the conceptualizing of international society and law into the conceptualizing of social process in general."[136] He sets himself the task of "providing, in the spirit of Kelsen, a basis of philosophical coherence for international society and law [whilst] ... integrating, in the spirit of McDougal, the international social process into social process more generally."[137]

Eunomia is written in a didactic, utopian tone and style. It is not an analytical study of thought and scholarship on the nature, theory and history of international law but a utopian blueprint for the "new international law." Allott declares "[t]he task of humanity now is to take possession of the wasteland of international society in the name of the people and in the name of justice ... redeem[ing] state-societies as systems for organizing the willing and acting of all human beings."[138] *Eunomia* includes three utopian draft treaties, each one invoking "We, the people":[139] "Treaty on the Constituting of International Society" (declaring "[i]international law [to be] ... the law of international society embodying the common interest of all humanity");[140] "Treaty on the Elimination of War" ("We undertake to do everything possible to eliminate the practice of war");[141] and "Treaty on the Elimination of Force in International Society" ("We undertake not to preach, teach, or otherwise propagate the idea that the use of force in international society is, or may be, politically or morally or legally justifiable, either in general or in particular situations").[142]

134 Ibid.
135 Ibid. xlvii.
136 Ibid. xlvii.
137 Ibid. xlviii.
138 Ibid. 254 (paragraph 14.1).
139 See opening lines of the three draft treaties at ibid. xxxv, xxxvii, and xxxviii.
140 Ibid. xxxv–xxxvii (quotation in brackets from Article 2 at xxxv).
141 Ibid. xxxvii–xxxviii (quotation in brackets from Article 2 at xxxvii).
142 Ibid. xxxviii–xl (quotation in brackets from Article 3 at xxxix).

Allott's concept of law is grounded in the deliberative, democratic participation of individuals, reflecting a classical public-ness that underpins the draft treaties:

> In generating the pure theory which contains the idea and the ideal of democracy, a society seeks the means to enable the people, the members of society, to embrace law as their own, not merely because they may conceive of themselves as its authorizing source but because they may will and act the law in their participation in the total social process which forms it.[143]

Allott's utopian plan is for all individuals to participate in the "self-creating of the people of the world through their own willing,"[144] bringing about "a self-willed change in human consciousness. A revolution, not in the streets but in the mind."[145] He describes this as "a practical theory of social idealism,"[146] insisting that "social idealism ... must become the basis for a new international law which humanity will construct as the law of a new international society."[147] Acknowledging that some regard *Eunomia* as "utopian, a dream rather than a prediction" because "it failed to specify the practical steps, especially the institutional changes, which would allow us to get ... from the actual to the ideal,"[148] Allott insists that "[w]hat we have made by thinking we can make new by new thinking."[149]

Allott's focus on thought excludes consideration of material circumstances, analysis of extant legal, social, political or economic structures, and historical inquiry. He offers various characterisations of what history is or its function in the ideational recreation of the world – "history is the past studying the past,"[150] "[h]istory is ... the story of a past and a future which are themselves a present-here-and-now,"[151] "[h]istory must be seen as the gradual actualizing of the potentiality of some original or pre-historical or putative society"[152] – without actually engaging with the detail of material history. This absence

143 Ibid. 256 (paragraph 14.7).
144 Ibid.
145 Ibid. 257 (paragraph 14.9).
146 Ibid. 410 (paragraph 19.25 – parts of the original text are in italics).
147 Ibid. 410–411 (paragraph 19.25 – parts of the original text are in italics).
148 Ibid. xxvii.
149 Ibid.
150 Ibid. 100 (paragraph 6.37).
151 Ibid. 192 (paragraph 12.36).
152 Ibid. 289 (paragraph 15.70).

suggests that Allott's social idealism operates in a temporal vacuum, outside history and the passage of time.[153]

Compounding this sense of detachment from what is and what was, *Eunomia* offers unsupported statements and verdicts in lieu of analysis of extant international law: "International law has been neither very threatening nor very useful to the politicians and the diplomats";[154] "The legal relations of international law were and are essentially the legal relations necessary to temper the public interactive willing and acting of the governments of statal societies as that willing and acting affects their sovereignty over territory."[155] No references to or quotations from literature are offered to support these claims – indeed, *Eunomia* contains no footnotes and no bibliography. This is more than a formal or presentational point. The absence of footnotes and a bibliography are, I suggest, a product of Allott's idealistic, blueprint utopianism. The argument for "self-creating" through thought does not,[156] for Allott, need to be situated in or connected to the world, to literature, or with the detail of what has been thought, what is being thought, or what is happening. Save for some prefatory reflections on globalisation, the professional experience of its author and the post-Cold War global situation,[157] *Eunomia* contains very little about time, place or lived experience, suggesting that such concerns do not arise when the world is viewed from "the cloisters of Cambridge."[158]

Eunomia's emphasis on thought and idealism and its exclusion of material and temporal concerns permeate Allott's other work.[159] He insists that "[s]ociety is made in the mind,"[160] that "[l]aw is a special way in which society thinks,"[161] and that "the ideal ... enables the human mind and human societies

153 See Carty, "Social Theory" (n. 124) 945: "The so-called different aspects of society, such as art, history, economics, religion, etc., all *exist* for Allott only as ideas in the mind of society. They do not impact upon reality as concrete or historical" (emphasis in original).

154 Allott, *Eunomia* (n. 11) 297 (paragraph 16.3).

155 Ibid. 296 (paragraph 16.2).

156 "Self-creating" – see Allott quotation at n. 144.

157 See Allott, *Eunomia* (n. 11) vii *et seq* ('Preface to the Paperback Edition') and xli *et seq* ('Preface').

158 See Allott quotation at n. 131.

159 See Carty, "Social Theory" (n. 124) 945: "Allott's model of idealist subjectivism dwarfs the ethical significance of the actual striving of the State governments of international society. There is a need to escape from the idealist trap of ethical perfectionism into the concrete struggle for ethical achievement."

160 Philip Allott, "Globalisation from above: Actualising the ideal through law" in Philip Allott, *The Health of Nations: Society and Law beyond the State* (Cambridge University Press, 2002) 70, 70 (original in italics).

161 Ibid. (original in italics).

to imagine a better future and to choose to enact a better future."[162] Allott's entire approach is defined by an insistence on the human-ness of reality: "Human beings inhabit a *human world*, entirely made by the human mind, a world parallel to the natural world, a self-made second human habitat, a human mind-world with its own *human reality*."[163]

There is, I suggest, a seamless connection between the didactic-idealist utopianism that drives Allott's work, the casual treatment of relevant theories and literature, and the absence of any substantive concern with time, place and lived experience. All are the product of an evangelical focus on the human-ness of reality, on human thought as the determinant of what is, what was, and what will be.[164] This suggests a return to the Enlightenment ideal of human thought as the supreme power, something Allott hints at in observing that "*Eunomia* and *Eutopia* simply ignore the End of Philosophy proclaimed in the twentieth century."[165]

Max Horkheimer and Theodor Adorno critique the idealist assumption of human power over reality and nature in *Dialectic of Enlightenment*, defining the aims of the Enlightenment in terms that resonate with Allott's project: "The program of the Enlightenment was the disenchantment of the world; the dissolution of myths and the substitution of knowledge for fancy."[166] The Enlightenment, for Horkheimer and Adorno, created a social, political and cultural situation in which "[w]ithout regard to distinctions, the world becomes subject to man":[167] "Man's likeness to God consists in sovereignty over existence, in the countenance of the law and master and in command."[168] By proudly "ignor[ing] the End of Philosophy" – and by "the End of philosophy" Allott seems to mean critical, post-Enlightenment, philosophy of the kind in which Horkheimer and Adorno engage – Allott seeks to wall his project off from critical thinking that contests the totalising supremacy of the human

162 Ibid.

163 Ibid. 75 (paragraph 3.11, emphasis in original).

164 See Martti Koskenniemi, "*Eunomia: New Order for a New World*" (review), (1993) 87 *American Journal of International Law* 160, 161: 'Ultimately, it is not society but human consciousness that is God [in *Eunomia*]; human consciousness projects everything there is, including time and space.'

165 Philip Allott, *Eutopia* (Edward Elgar, 2016) ix; see also Koskenniemi, "*Eunomia*" (n. 164) 162, describing *Eunomia* (n. 11) as "unabashedly nonmodern … [and as reflecting] a sense that modernity has gone astray."

166 Theodor W. Adorno and Max Horkheimer, "The Concept of Enlightenment" in Theodor W. Adorno and Max Horkheimer, *Dialectic of Enlightenment* (Verso, 1997, [1944]) 3, 3.

167 Ibid. 8.

168 Ibid. 9

mind. It is difficult to understand why Allott, as a scholar writing in the late twentieth and early twenty-first century, would imagine he can "simply ignore" the development of post-Enlightenment philosophy.

On Horkheimer and Adorno's interpretation Francis Bacon, to whom Allott refers,[169] advocates a "patriarchal" state of "concordance between the mind and man and the nature of things" in which "the human mind ... overcomes superstition [and] ... hold[s] sway over a disenchanted nature."[170] This "concordance" means that "[k]nowledge, which is power, knows no obstacles: neither in the enslavement of men nor in compliance with the world's rulers."[171] Such totalising knowledge originates in a fear of the unknown:

> Man imagines himself free from fear when there is no longer anything unknown ... Enlightenment is mythic fear turned radical ... Nothing at all may remain outside, because the mere idea of outsideness is the very source of fear.[172]

Human dominance over nature and reality naturalises itself over time: "The more the machinery of thought subjects existence to itself, the more blind its resignation in reproducing existence. Hence enlightenment returns to mythology, which it never really knew how to elude."[173] The prevailing logic is one of domination as "men [sic.] distance themselves from nature in order thus imaginatively to present it to themselves – but only in order to determine how it is to be dominated."[174]

Allott's attachment to the Enlightenment values of knowledge and rationality critiqued by Horkheimer and Adorno is again on display in *Eutopia*. Published in 2016 as something like a sequel to *Eunomia*, Allott describes the book as "designed to bring the great and ancient existential human debate back to life, before it is too late."[175] Invoking Thomas More's *Utopia* and Francis Bacon – in particular Bacon's insistence that "a revolution in our understanding of the human mind could produce every other kind of revolution"[176] – the

169 See text at n. 176 below.
170 Adorno and Horkheimer, "The Concept of Enlightenment" (n. 166) 4.
171 Ibid.
172 Ibid. 16.
173 Ibid. 27.
174 Ibid. 39.
175 Allott, *Eutopia* (n. 165) ix.
176 Ibid. vii–viii.

book's foreword closes with a quotation from More: "Deservedly ought I to be called by the name of Eutopia or Happy Land."[177]

Eutopia claims to offer a "road from Isotpia to Eutopia – from where we are to where we want to be – pass[ing] through Knowtopia."[178] Knowtopia is "the place where we learn about the extraordinary powers of the human mind, the private mind and the public mind, and where we take stock of the human condition ... the bright face and the dark face of human history ... our present troubled situation and our perilous future."[179] In a didactic-idealist tone familiar from *Eunomia*, Allott claims that in *Eutopia* "[w]e have learned that, over the course of millennia and in countless different cultures, the human mind and the human will have been wonderfully creative and ingenious and bold in responding to an unceasing succession of challenges."[180]

Allott is unwilling to allow the reader to formulate her own response to the text, preferring to tell us what "[w]e have learned."[181] This desire to control the readership is also apparent in passages unsupported by reasoning and lacking any attempt at persuasion. Consider, for example, this passage on the function of art:

> Bad art and popular culture give pleasure to many people, and they make money for those who create and manage and sell them. That is justification enough for bad art and popular culture. And popular culture can sometimes rise to the level of high art.[182]

Employing a similar approach, Allott notes (in a chapter entitled "Paradoxes of Being Human II") that "[t]here is no agreement among biologists and ethnologists as to the general 'nature' of our animal ancestors and hence no agreement as to the instincts that we have inherited."[183] No details on the biological and ethnological literature consulted in formulating this view are offered, and this lack of support and reasoning recurs throughout the text – see, for example,

177 Ibid. ix.
178 Ibid. 289 (paragraph 12.1).
179 Ibid.
180 Ibid. (paragraph 12.2).
181 Martti Koskenniemi, "International Law as Therapy: Reading the Health of Nations" (2005) 16 *European Journal of International Law* 329, at 331, notes an "aesthetics of *grandeur*" in Allott's work, suggesting, at 332, that "[s]omething more takes place here than mere argument. The style invites the reader to step into the stream of history, something like the Palace of Versailles, to participate in the conversation of humankind that is taking place here."
182 Allott, *Eutopia* (n. 165) 111 (paragraph 6.52).
183 Ibid. 53 (paragraph 4.5).

the assertion that "[w]hat people most want is to be left in command of a private space in which they and their family can flourish, within a public space designed to deliver, and actually delivering the best possible conditions for personal flourishing."[184] No empirical support for this assertion is offered, nor does Allott justify his preference for a liberal-capitalist "command of a private space" model over more communal, collectivist forms of living.

Eutopia, like *Eunomia*, has neither footnotes nor bibliography. Instead, each chapter is followed by a list of "other voices" – that is, voices other than Allott's – including Shakespeare, Rousseau, Machiavelli, Thomas More, Hegel, Nietzsche, Alexander Pope, Einstein, Wikipedia, Freud, Marx, and Kant. Whilst some non-European "other voices" are included – a quotation from Hsun Ch'ing,[185] a reference to Franz Fanon[186] – there is a strong bias towards modern or pre-modern socio-political theory and philosophy written by European men. Allott could have recognised and engaged with the voices and perspectives of others in his text, highlighting sources or influences on his thinking, but he prefers to position "other voices" in lists of quotations that the reader comes to only after reading his text, granting his voice primacy.

Allott's assertive, even domineering mode of authorship, serves as a means of effecting "[a utopian] revolution ... in the mind" of the reader.[187] This contrasts with more collaborative understandings of the relationship between author and reader, such as that outlined by Walter Benjamin in "The Author as Producer."[188] Benjamin advocates an authorial style in which "the reader is at all times ready to become a writer – that is, a describer, or even a prescriber."[189] Authors must "never ... merely work on products but always, at the same time, work on the means of production."[190] This "*Umfunktionierung*" or "functional transformation" in the production of text means that "the conventional distinction between author and the public ... begins ... to disappear."[191] The point of writing, for Benjamin, is "to induce other producers to produce" and "to put an improved apparatus at their disposal."[192] The "apparatus" will be "better, the more consumers it is able to turn into producers – that is, readers or spectators

184 Ibid. 83 (paragraph 5.18).
185 Ibid. 198.
186 Ibid. 321.
187 "Revolution ... in the mind" – see Allott quotation at n. 145 above.
188 Walter Benjamin, "The Author as Producer" in Michael W. Jennings, Howard Eiland and Gary Smith (eds.), *Walter Benjamin: Selected Writings, Volume 2, part 2, 1931–1934* (Belknap Press of Harvard University Press, 2005) 768.
189 Ibid. 771.
190 Ibid. 777.
191 Ibid., at 774 (on "*Umfunktionierung*"), and at 771 (on "conventional distinction").
192 Ibid. 777.

into collaborators."[193] In promoting "*Umfunktionierung*" Benjamin critiques the alternative perspective of "Activism" whose "demands are summed up ... in plain language" as "'rule of the mind'" or "'rule of the intellectuals.'"[194] According to Benjamin the activist "intellectual" is "a type of person defined by his opinions, attitudes or dispositions, but not by his position in the process of production."[195] Whilst the activist intellectual writes "political manifestos" the practitioner of *Umfunktionierung* "eliminate[s] the antithesis ... between performers and listeners."[196]

Allott's didactic style positions him as very much the "performer" and he consistently tells his reader or "listener" what is, what ought to be, and what the reader ought to think,[197] claiming the capacity to define *the* human experience of reality,[198] and even "[t]he task of humanity."[199] He speaks for his readership, for "we" and of "us,"[200] denying the reader the space to form her own views as she reads. This is not "*Umfunktionierung*," not an exchange between author and reader that generates productive capacity in its readership, but a controlling and unpersuasive process of blunt, authoritarian instruction.[201]

---

193 Ibid.

194 Ibid. 772

195 Ibid. 773.

196 Ibid. 772, 775.

197 See Allott, *Eutopia* (n. 165), 209: "Law *is* the anatomy and physiology of a society" (emphasis added).

198 See Allott, *Eunomia* (n. 11), chapter 8 ("The Dimensions of Reality"), 123–132.

199 Ibid. 254: "The task of humanity now is to take possession of the waste-land of international society in the name of the people and in the name of justice, to redeem state-societies as systems for organizing the willing and acting of all human beings."

200 See, for example, Allott, *Eutopia* (n. 165) 149: "We are ruled by the power of memory. We are ruled by the power of imagination. We are ruled by the power of knowledge. And we are ruled by the power of *emotion*" (emphasis in original); ibid. 298: "We are worker bees who built the hive we live in, but hardly enjoy the honey that collectively we produce"; ibid. 226: "The behaviour of governments in the twentieth century taught us a painful lesson – evolutionary constitutionalism, the Rule of Law, fundamental constitutional rights, and the miracle of law-making in implementation of a society's high-values were not enough to control gross abuse of power by governments."

201 See Carty "Social Theory" (n. 124) 939: "If one cannot identify with or imagine oneself as communicating with a particular audience, it may be understandable that one's work contains no references. With Allott this means the reader is left guessing what Allott himself has read and even left wondering whether he is 'supposed' to be reading the work. However, the confident tone of the oracle runs through *Eunomia*, leaving the reader with the sense that 'the fault' must lie with him." See also Koskenniemi, "International Law as Therapy" (n. 181), at 340: "His appeal to us is the same as the appeal of a clergyman showing his congregation how far they have strayed from the good path, who speaks again of sin and redemption and all the horrors of hell and thus makes us feel spiritualized as

This style of blueprint utopianism has been critiqued for its tendency towards messianism and totalitarianism. Russell Jacoby traces this critique back to Thomas More's original *Utopia*, written in 1515 and 1516.[202] Tracking the development of More's life and work in England, from apparently advocating freedom of religion and conscience in *Utopia*, to "hunt[ing] and pursu[ing] Protestants and heretics" and banning books,[203] Jacoby rejects Jasper Ridley's charge that More became "'a fanatic determined to crush what he considers to be the forces of evil'" on the basis that "[Ridley] uses twentieth-century categories to damn More."[204] Whatever the merits of Ridley's charge, there is a troubling connection between More's absolutism and Allott's absolute confidence in human-ness and human thought.

Jacoby's analysis of anti-utopianism extends, beyond critiques of More, to Karl Popper's work.[205] Popper critiques the view that "rational political action must be based upon a more or less clear and detailed description or blueprint of our ideal state, and also upon a plan or blueprint of the historical path that leads towards this goal."[206] For Popper such blueprint utopianism is "an all too attractive theory … [that is] dangerous … pernicious … [and] self-defeating, and it leads to violence."[207] For Popper there is no way to determine the "ideal state" through argumentation, reasoning, or science,[208] so arguments about the ideal state "will at least partly have the character of religious differences."[209] To achieve his preferred ideal state:

> the Utopianist must win over, or else crush … competitors who do not share his own Utopian aims … He has to be very thorough in eliminating and stamping out all heretical competing views … [T]he rationality of his political action demands constancy of aim for a long time ahead; and

we leave the church to lead our private and professional lives as we have always done. Of course, this is a valuable service. But it is not a revolutionary service."

202 Jacoby (n. 3) 44.

203 Ibid. 44–45.

204 Ibid. 48.

205 Ibid. 52–58.

206 Karl Popper, "Utopia and Violence" (1986) 149(1) *World Affairs* 3, 5, discussed by Jacoby (n. 3) at 56–57.

207 Popper ibid.

208 Ibid. 6: "Since we cannot determine the ultimate ends of political actions scientifically, or by purely rational methods, differences of opinion concerning what the ideal state should be like cannot always be smoothed out by the method of argument."

209 Ibid.

> this can only be achieved if he not merely crushes competing Utopian religions, but as far as possible stamps out all memory of them.[210]

On this basis "Utopian rationalism.... [h]owever benevolent its ends ... does not bring happiness, but only the familiar misery of being condemned to live under a tyrannical government."[211] Isaiah Berlin is similarly opposed to radical means. According to Jacoby, "Berlin ratifies an inherent and irreducible pluralism that gives the lie to any utopian theorizing,"[212] opposing ambitious plans on the basis that "[w]e should be wary of 'drastic action, in personal life or in public policy' ... since they may lead to unanticipated suffering."[213]

Hannah Arendt is the last in Jacoby's group of 'liberal anti-utopians.'[214] Jacoby highlights the proximity between Popper's and Arendt's positions, noting Arendt's observation that "[t]he aggressiveness of totalitarianism springs not from the lust for power ... nor for profit, but only for ideological reasons: to make the world consistent, to prove that its respective supersense has been right."[215] Arendt's, Berlin's and Popper's perspectives are connected by their fear of totalisation. Allott's work simply ignores that well-founded fear, concealing the link between utopianism, totalisation / totalitarianism behind superficially appealing calls for the constitution of a truly inter-national society.[216]

Susan Marks' analysis of "false contingency" offers a corrective to the superficiality of Allott's idealistic utopianism, insisting that "[w]hile current arrangements can indeed be changed, change unfolds within a context that includes systemic constraints and pressures."[217] Marks explains that she wants to "re-evoke ... the idea that things can be, and quite frequently are, contingent without being random, accidental, or arbitrary,"[218] "us[ing] the term 'false contingency' to denote the failure to take that idea adequately into account."[219] Marks does not consider Allott's work in her treatment of international legal "false contingency," but Allott does seem to treat "the injustices of the present order ... as though they were random, accidental and arbitrary,"[220] as though they can simply be thought away.

---

210 Ibid.
211 Ibid. 7.
212 Jacoby (n. 3) 67.
213 Ibid. 68.
214 Ibid. 75.
215 Ibid. 76.
216 See the draft treaties in Allott, *Eunomia* (n. 11) xxxv–xl.
217 Susan Marks, "False Contingency" (2009) 62 *Current Legal Problems* 1, 2.
218 Ibid.
219 Ibid.
220 Ibid. 20.

My critique of Koskenniemi's and Cassese's brand of blueprint utopianism was that they are hidebound by an emphasis on what is that excludes the possibility of what might be and, as a consequence, altogether too much "within" existing international law. My critique of Allott's ideational blueprint utopianism is that it operates too much 'outside' extant international law, material reality and history. For a scholar so attached to Enlightenment ideals,[221] Allott's work is surprisingly postmodern. Consistent with what Jameson sees as a postmodern "crisis in historicity,"[222] Allott casts material reality and history aside in order to sell *his* utopian vision of the human-ness of reality in a process of "absolute self-reproduction"[223] – that is, his own "self-reproduction." Allott sells *his* view of "a human mind-world with its own *human reality*,"[224] as seen "from the cloisters of Cambridge,"[225] *via* a didactic tone and an attempt to control his audience. References and history and literature would only get in the way when the objective is aesthetic appeal to present-day audiences *via* numbered paragraphs (all of *Eunomia*'s and *Eutopia*'s paragraphs are numbered).[226]

Allott's "human reality" treats all reality, past, present and future, as a postmodern commodity for humans to consume as they re-order global society, locking international law into the "eternal present" of a postmodernity in which commodification and consumption rule.[227] If the lesson of climate change is that humans are only too capable of commodifying and consuming then, if international law is to have any hope of addressing climate change, the absolute commodification of reality entailed by Allott's Eutopianism must be confined to its home in Cambridge.

4 *Samuel Moyn's Blueprint for Human Rights*

Across three books,[228] and in one collection of essays,[229] Samuel Moyn argues that "international human rights … should find a better compromise between utopianism and realism than has thus far been realized,"[230] insisting that "if

---

221 See text at n. 165 to n. 177.

222 See text at n. 35.

223 See text at n. 36.

224 See text at n. 163.

225 See text at n. 131.

226 On "aesthetic appeal" see text (including Jameson quotation) at n. 40.

227 "Eternal present" – see text at n. 45.

228 Moyn, *The Last Utopia* (n. 12); Samuel Moyn, *Christian Human Rights* (University of Pennsylvania Press, 2015); Samuel Moyn, *Not Enough: Human Rights in an Unequal World* (Belknap Press of Harvard University Press, 2018).

229 Samuel Moyn, *Human Rights and the Uses of History* (Verso, 2014).

230 Samuel Moyn, "Epilogue: The Future of Human Rights" in Moyn, *Human Rights and the Uses of History* (Verso, 2014) 135, 136.

the human rights movement does not offer a more realistic and politicized utopia, something else will take its place."[231] Moyn argues that human rights "need to descend into the programmatic contest for power" and "become more scientific" because "a politics of human rights ... should engage in the programmatic concern with designing good states, for the sake of global economic welfare."[232] Moyn flirts with iconoclastic utopianism, *via* a "return to the utopian imagination in its pure form, divorced from attempts to institutionalize it,"[233] contemplating the idea that we should "proceed from the refusal to pay reality the respect of conforming to it."[234] The flirtation is short-lived, however, and Moyn prefers a politicized human rights practice that builds Utopia out of existing reality whilst, at the same time, contesting that reality.[235]

Moyn's outline programme for the future of human rights grows out of his critique of contemporary human rights discourse and law:[236] indeed, his critique is developed more extensively, across his three books, than his positive programme. In his first book, *The Last Utopia: Human Rights in History,* Moyn offers "[a]n alternative history of human rights, with a much more recent timeline" than conventional accounts focussed on the post-World War Two era.[237] Moyn argues that "[o]ver the course of the 1970s, the moral world of Westerners shifted, opening a space for the sort of utopianism that coalesced in an international human rights movement that had never existed before."[238] Critiquing

231 Ibid. 146.

232 Ibid. 142, 146

233 Ibid. 135.

234 Ibid. 136.

235 See ibid. 136: "[M]y worry is that human rights have conformed too much to reality. The utopian challenge presented by human rights has proved so minimal that they easily became neutered, and were even invoked as excuses – for example, in wars serving other interests – for choices their original advocates did not intend." See also ibid. at 142–143: "[T]hey [human rights] seem often to make little practical difference, amounting to an ornament on a tragic world. Because they are not realistic enough, they end up accommodating reality too much. A better compromise between utopianism and realism is required."

236 On the outline nature of this programme see ibid. 143: "A better compromise between utopianism and realism is required. How to find this compromise is anything but obvious. But it may help to conclude with a list of theses that indicate the sort of compromise I have in mind." Moyn's list, at ibid. 143–147, includes "[a] politics of human rights must transcend judges" and "A politics of human rights must seek power over the real conditions of enjoyment of formal entitlements."

237 Moyn, *The Last Utopia* (n. 12) 7.

238 Ibid. 1.

the "formalism" and "minimalism" of 1970s human rights utopianism,[239] Moyn argues that human rights became extra-political:

> One of the distinctive features of human rights consciousness in the crucial years of the 1970s was that appeal to morality could seem pure even where politics had shown itself to be a soiled and impossible domain ... Human rights were preferable because they were strategically necessary and practically feasible, but also because they were morally pure. The disavowal of earlier utopias [of a more overtly political or revolutionary nature] took place in part out of the aspiration to achieve through a moral critique of politics the sense of a pure cause that had once been sought in politics itself.[240]

I am concerned with Moyn's blueprint utopianism and not with the accuracy of his historical analysis. The critique in *The Last Utopia* is that post-1970s human rights utopianism is more an outline sketch than a detailed blueprint: "[I]n the confusing tumult of 1970s social movements ... [human rights] became bound up with the widespread desire to drop utopia and have one anyway."[241] Moyn's problem with sketches is that they lack political content and programmatic detail. On his analysis it was the development of a distinctively formal, minimalist human rights culture in the 1970s that made human rights suited to the formalities of law. The alliance between human rights and international law is, on Moyn's analysis, a story about formalised 1970s human rights coming to international law, rather than international law acquiring a substantive commitment to human rights values.[242]

On Moyn's account "even if their breakthrough [in the 1970s] depended on their antipolitics" in post-1970s cultural and social conditions "partisans of the human rights idea were forced to confront the need for political agenda and programmatic vision – the very things whose absence allowed for their utopia

239 On formalism and international law see ibid. 210, and for a critique of minimalism see ibid. 172.

240 Moyn, *The Last Utopia* (n. 12) 170–171.

241 Ibid. 175.

242 See ibid. 210: "The turn by dissidents like Aleksandr-Esenin-Volpin and Václav Havel to human rights was also, and explicitly, a revival or the plausibility of abstract norms as a vehicle of moral progress; and though they owed the general intellectual renewal of formalism to arguments by Eastern European dissidents, it was fateful that international lawyers were the existing custodians of international legal forms to which those very figures appealed. The lawyers had husbanded formalism without rights during an era of realist dominance. But they were the natural inheritors of a reactivated formalism revolving around the rights they had earlier marginalized."

to emerge so spectacularly and discontinuously in the first place."[243] Certainly by the 1990s, with "revelations of the Cambodian genocide ... [and] the mid-1990s resurgence of 'ethnic cleansing',"[244] 1970s style formalist-minimalist human rights thinking was (apparently) in trouble: "From having triumphed because it lacked a political blueprint, the human rights movement was forced to draw up plans to remedy a crisis-ridden world."[245]

Having critiqued the sketchy nature of 1970s and post-1970s human rights utopianism for much of the book, Moyn performs a partial *volte-face* towards the end of *The Last Utopia*, asking (and not answering the question of) whether human rights "should restrict themselves to offering minimal constraints on responsible politics, not a new form of maximal politics of their own."[246] Any doubts about Moyn's commitment to programmatic, blueprint utopianism evaporate by 2012 when – perhaps surprisingly, given the post-9/11 U.S. experience in Afghanistan and Iraq – he calls for human rights to "engage in the programmatic concern with designing good states, for the sake of global economic welfare."[247]

Readers have to wait for 2018's *Not Enough*, however, to get a sense of the blueprint Moyn favours, with his second book – 2015's *Christian Human Rights* – simply expanding and consolidating the critique. *The Last Utopia* argued that the true origin of human rights' social and political prominence lay in the 1970s and not the 1940s. In a similar vein *Christian Human Rights* argues that connections between Christianity and human rights, particularly in the 1930s and 1940s, are not a mere aspect of human rights history – as much of the existing scholarship, on Moyn's analysis, suggests – but central to that history.[248]

Moyn contests the orthodox idea that liberal democratic values were expressed in and through "the annunciation of human rights in the 1940s,"[249] in a manner consistent with a revolutionary tradition stretching back to the

---

243 Ibid. 213.

244 Ibid. 220.

245 Ibid. 221.

246 Ibid. 227.

247 Moyn, "Epilogue" (n. 230) 146.

248 Moyn, *Christian Human Rights* (n. 228) 4: "Mainstream observers are generally unaware of – for their secular historians have nervously bypassed – the Christian incarnation of human rights, which interferes with their preferred understandings of today's highest principles. Meanwhile, those interested in Christian sources, overwhelmingly Christians themselves, are prone to misinterpret them. The proposition that human rights arose with profound connections to Christian contexts is normally defended, in both public discourse and scholarly arguments, in a highly abstract way and about long ago events."

249 Ibid. 8.

French Revolution and "*droits de l'homme*."[250] He argues that "through this lost and misremembered transwar era, it is equally if not more viable to regard human rights as a project of the Christian right, not the secular left."[251] Moyn approaches the 1940s as a period in which "the Christian right" succeeded in making a break with an earlier, revolutionary tradition of rights as a challenge to orthodoxy, order and the state. A conservative rights tradition emerged out of that break and for Moyn that tradition "haunts politics to this day, as the deepest aspirations of democracy changed [in the 1940s], prizing moderation against extremes over liberation of human capacity and restoring order to its regrettable if time-honored status as the centrepiece of justice."[252]

Moyn seeks to demonstrate the practicalities of this haunting, arguing that the Christian origins of the European human rights architecture, codified in the European Convention on Human Rights, are reflected in recent decisions by the European Court of Human Rights endorsing restrictions on the wearing of the burqa and niqab in France, Switzerland and Turkey.[253] For Moyn these cases:

> owe part of their doctrinal rationale and perhaps their exclusionary implications not to the secularist associations of religious freedom but to the legacy of the religious struggle against communism once feared as secularism incarnate. The Muslim has taken the place of the communist in the contemporary European imagination.[254]

---

250 Ibid., and see also ibid. 9: "This book on the origins of Christian human rights therefore focuses most of all on the extent to which, across the 1930s and 1940s, the language of rights was extricated from the legacy of the French Revolution, the secularist mantle of which the Soviet leaders were now widely seen to have assumed. And thanks to the championship of rights within a new political formation – constitutionally organized religious democracy governed by Christian parties – a compromise between Christianity and democracy became not only palatable but a precious resource for the future of religious values."

251 Ibid. 8.

252 Ibid. 24.

253 See *Belgin Dogru v France* (2008) 39 EHRR 179; *Dahlab v Switzerland*, Application No 42393/98, unreported, <http://hudoc.echr.coe.int/sites/eng/pages/search.aspx?i=001-22643#{"itemid":["001-22643"]}>; *Leyla Sahin v Turkey* (2007) 44 EHRR 99; *SAS v France*, (2015) 60 EHRR 244. These cases are analysed by Moyn, *Christian Human Rights* (n. 228), at 137–138 and 142–145. For my analysis of these cases (with the exception of *Belgin Dogru*) see Matthew Nicholson, "Majority Rule and Human Rights: Identity and Non-Identity in SAS v France" (2016) 67(2) *Northern Ireland Legal Quarterly* 115.

254 Moyn, *Christian Human Rights* (n. 228) 145.

He insists that "[i]f the human rights movement does not improve states – or even the hearts of the men and women that Christianity at its most ambitious and inspiring promised to transform – it will demand replacement, in the name of its own ideals or some better ones."[255] This conclusion, like the argument of *The Last Utopia*, is underpinned by a programmatic, utopian desire for tangible progress.

In 2018's *Not Enough* Moyn moves from arguing, in *The Last Utopia* and *Christian Human Rights*, for the value of pragmatic, blueprint utopianism as a response to the deficiencies and exclusions of extant human rights, to the presentation of an actual blueprint for the future of human rights:

> [M]y goal is to stake out a moderate position between those who claim that human rights are unrelated to political economy and distributive injustice (except of course to provide the essential tools for reining them in) and those who think the human rights revolution has been a mere sham masking inhumane domination.[256]

Moyn opposes an idea of human rights that limits their purpose to the satisfaction of basic needs, advocating the pursuit of true equality: "Human rights, focused on securing enough for everyone, are essential – but they are not enough."[257] His argument develops in stages. First, the reader is invited to consider France's 1793–1794 Jacobin state and its management of the economy on the basis (to borrow Moyn's quotation from Harold Laski) that "'distinctions of wealth are legislative creations, and that, where crisis demands it, egalitarian innovation may be deliberately attempted.'"[258] Next, Moyn argues for a "reread[ing]" of the Universal Declaration of Human Rights as an instrument "connected with the believable empowerment and intervention of the state" in opposition to free-market, neoliberal readings of the UDHR an instrument supportive of "the prestige of non-governmental action or the cautious reform of judges."[259] Analysis of Franklin Delano Roosevelt's mid-1940s effort to refocus American social policy on socio-economic rights follows,[260] with the International Covenant on Economic Social and Cultural Rights ('ICESCR')

255 Ibid. 181.
256 Moyn, *Not Enough* (n. 228) xi.
257 Ibid. 8.
258 Ibid. 23 (quoting Harold Laski).
259 Ibid. 44.
260 Ibid., chapter three.

receiving rather less attention than might be thought necessary in a book about global socio-economic equality.[261]

Moyn considers the New International Economic Order – a 1970s programme of action by newly independent states in the global South, seeking to address global economic imbalances between former imperial states in the global North and newly independent states in the global South – in sections of a chapter that also covers the post-war decolonization and the post-war fortunes of the International Labour Organisation.[262] As Julieta Lemaitre observes, the structure of *Not Enough* suggests that for Moyn there is the U.S. and "the rest of the world."[263] That seems to explain why Moyn covers the NIEO – a collective, collaborative global South effort – in parts of a chapter that comes immediately after an entire chapter on mid-1940s U.S. socio-economic policy.[264]

Critique of the "turn away from socialism" in Amnesty International's and Human Rights Watch's work accompanies a negative review of Robert McNamara's late-60s / early-70s World Bank presidency and his focus on alleviating "absolute poverty" rather than promoting equality.[265] Expressing qualified agreement with Susan Marks and Naomi Klein, Moyn's final chapter attacks the complicit relationship between human rights and neoliberalism, setting up an epilogue centred on the figure of "a modern Croesus" – the original Croesus being a fabulously wealthy Ancient Greek king – who "insists on

261 John Finnis, "On Moyn's Christian Human Rights" (2017) 28(1) *King's Law Journal* 12, at 13 (footnote 2) critiques Moyn's lack of attention (in *The Last Utopia* (n. 12) and *Christian Human Rights* (n. 228)) to the International Covenant on Civil and Political Rights and the ICESCR. Antony Anghie, "Whose Utopia? Human Rights, Development and the Third World" (2013) 22(1) *Qui Parle* 63, 69 notes Moyn's cursory treatment of the ICCPR and ISESCR in *The Last Utopia* (n. 12).

262 See Moyn, *Not Enough* (n. 228) chapter 4, "Globalizing Welfare after Empire."

263 See Julieta Lemaitre, "The View from Somewhere: on Samuel Moyn's Not Enough," 9th July 2018, *Law and Political Economy* <https://lpeblog.org/2018/07/09/the-view-from-somewhere-on-samuel-moyns-not-enough/> (last visited 2nd August 2019), describing *Not Enough* as "deliciously U.S.-centric, in spite of the author's effort in mentioning 'the rest of the world' so obviously excluded from the 'we' which sometimes appears. Seen from South America, the effort at inclusion is shockingly thin: only one line about the Mexican constitution in a book on social and economic rights in the world (compare to ten pages on some guy called Beitz) and basically nothing on agrarian reform or on indigenous land rights or the role of the ILO in their defense. The ferocious debates over health rights litigation, or on the real effects of structural litigation on the provision of public good are also largely absent from *Not Enough*." Lemaitre, ibid., also comments: "It would be perhaps too much to ask for the historical to acknowledge the limits of what can be seen from New York, or what can be understood from New York about 'the rest of the world.'"

264 See Moyn, *Not Enough* (n. 228) chapter 3 ("FDR's Second Bill").

265 Ibid. 122–123, 131–133.

a floor of protection, so that everyone living under his benevolent but total ascendency can escape destitution."[266]

For Moyn this "modern Croesus" embodies the situation of contemporary human rights: "We increasingly live in Croesus's world."[267] The force of this argument is, perhaps, diminished by global financier George Soros' endorsement on the book's back cover ("[i]f we don't address the growing global phenomenon of economic inequality, the human rights movement as we know it cannot survive or flourish") but, nevertheless, the book ends with a call to detach human rights from neoliberalism.[268]

Pankaj Mishra, reviewing *Not Enough* in the *London Review of Books*, comments that "Moyn wants to reinstate socialism ... as an ethical ideal and political objective."[269] The book starts with reflections on the legacy of Jacobinism – a statist, central-management approach to social and economic affairs – and ends with a George Soros-endorsed indictment of the super-rich, so Mishra seems to be right. Moyn's blueprint is, ultimately, anti-neoliberalism (formalism and minimalism) and pro-socialism (equality and statism). It is built on a critique of the particularity and biases of extant human rights (the particular targets in *The Last Utopia* and *Not Enough* are formalism and minimalism, and, in *Christian Human Rights*, the *faux*-universalism of a human rights tradition in which Christianity has exerted significant but often overlooked influence).

The charge against Allott, outlined above, is that he secures the coherence and appeal of his utopian blueprint by omitting relevant literature and ignoring history.[270] The similar charge against Moyn is that his blueprint for the future of human rights achieves its coherence and contemporary appeal by preferring the *status quo* to radical change, limiting its ambition to what can 'realistically' be achieved within the current human rights system and ignoring the detail of the context in which that system operates. Considered together, Allott's and Moyn's work illustrate a central tension in blueprint utopianism. The blueprint will always be either too ambitious and consequently unrealistic (Allott), or too realistic and consequently lacking in ambition (Moyn).

266 Ibid. 212.

267 Ibid. 212.

268 Ibid. 220: "Human rights emerged as the highest morality of an unequal world, in a neoliberal circumstance its partisans could struggle to humanize, only to find themselves accused of complicity with it. Human rights activists should not desire that companionship, even if they decide that their role is not to argue for equality ... Human rights will return to their defensible importance only as soon as humanity saves itself from its low ambitions."

269 Pankaj Mishra, "The Mask It Wears" (2018) 40(12) *London Review of Books* 9, 13.

270 See text at n. 226.

Equally, to make itself appealing to an audience the blueprint will necessarily omit, to a greater or lesser extent, aspects of the context in which it is situated in the form of relevant literature, significant history, contemporary events, or competing perspectives. There will, then, in the design of a utopian blueprint, always be too much or too little ambition, too much or too little detail. A review of the ambition and detail critiques as applied to Moyn's work – the focus of the next section – illustrates the necessary limitations of blueprint utopianism in general.

4.1 Ambition and Detail

Paul O'Connell, reviewing *Not Enough*, argues in iconoclastic terms that "[t]he fundamental problem … is not neoliberalism, or poor distributional choices (though of course both matter), but the structural character of the extant social system."[271] He is troubled by Moyn's "resign[ation] to the idea that there is nothing beyond capitalism,"[272] claiming that "in continuing to treat capitalism as an unquestioned, perennial premise [Moyn's] critique is, itself, not enough."[273] Zak Manfredi makes a similar point, asking whether, "[a]fter nearly four decades of neoliberal hegemony, we might … pause to ask: is a (re)turn to the welfare state the most left political forces can hope for?"[274]

Gráinne de Búrca critiques Moyn's ambition from a different perspective, claiming that it is not – as O'Connell and Manfredi charge – lacking, but mis-directed. For de Búrca Moyn's pre-occupation with the "human rights movement" is "rather … odd" because "the system of capitalism" and "its more recent political incarnation in the guise of global and domestic neoliberalism" are, on de Búrca's analysis, "among the root causes of the material inequality with which [Moyn] is concerned."[275] de Búrca suggests that Moyn ought to make capitalism and neoliberalism "the target of [his] ire,"[276] assuming the very separation between neoliberalism and human rights that *Not Enough*

271 Paul O'Connell, "Capitalism, Inequality and Human Rights," 4th June 2018, *Law and Political Economy* <https://lpeblog.org/2018/06/04/capitalism-inequality-and-human-rights/> (last visited 2nd August 2019).

272 Ibid.

273 Ibid.

274 Zak Manfredi, "Compatibility as Complicity? On Neoliberalism and Human Rights," 28th May 2018, *Law and Political Economy* <https://lpeblog.org/2018/05/28/compatibility-as-complicity-on-neoliberalism-and-human-rights/#more-707> (last visited 2nd August 2019).

275 Gráinne de Búrca, "Samuel Moyn, *Not Enough: Human Rights in an Unequal World*" (review) (2018) 16(4) *International Journal of Constitutional Law* 1347, 1347.

276 Ibid.

seeks to problematize.[277] There is, of course, no 'right' answer to the question of whether there is a human rights system and a separate capitalist / neoliberal system. That seems to be de Búrca's view, with O'Connell preferring the notion of one global, capitalist system that has a human rights component. Moyn holds neither of these views:

> [M]y goal is to stake out a moderate position between those who claim that human rights are unrelated to political economy and distributive injustice (except of course to provide the essential tools for reining them in) and those who think the human rights revolution has been a mere sham masking inhumane domination.[278]

O'Connell's insistence on "the structural character of the extant social system" comes close to the latter view ("the human rights revolution has been a mere sham masking inhumane domination"), and de Búrca's bifurcated analysis of "the human rights movement" and "the system of capitalism" comes close to "claim[ing] that human rights are unrelated to political economy." Moyn insists that human rights can and must pursue global equality by challenging capitalism's distributional effects, perceiving two inter-connected systems – capitalism and human rights – with human rights, at their best, serving as a check on the functioning of the capitalist machine.

O'Connell goes beyond Moyn's two overlapping systems, insisting that everything in "the extant social system" is capitalism, whilst de Búrca objects to what she sees as Moyn's attack on human rights because capitalism is, for her, the more appropriate punch bag. Moyn fully appreciates the potency of the conservative (de Búrca) and radical (O'Connell) perspectives – hence his definition of *Not Enough*'s "goal" in terms of a "moderate position" – and, responding to O'Connell, defends his moderacy:

> Karl Marx's central mistake ... was his belief [which, Moyn implies, O'Connell shares] in take-it-or-leave-it 'systems' of production, exchange, and distribution when political history and legal theory since suggest that what we are really dealing with are makeshift and ramshackle assemblages with radically different outcomes for participants.[279]

---

277 On Moyn's construction of the relationship between human rights and neoliberalism see quotation in n. 268.

278 Moyn, *Not Enough* (n. 228) xi (also quoted at n. 256).

279 Sam Moyn, "Bias and Exclusion in Human Rights History," 13th August 2018, *Law and Political Economy* <https://lpeblog.org/2018/08/13/bias-and-exclusion-in-human-rights-history/> (last visited 2nd August 2019).

The disagreement between de Búrca, Moyn and O'Connell is a case of the conservative, the radical and the moderate talking past each other because they subscribe to divergent social and political theories. No resolution of the background theoretical tension is possible, but the three perspectives can be evaluated in terms of what they make possible.

de Búrca invokes the ideal of a "revitalized democratic system" and,[280] maintaining her insistence on the separateness of systems, claims:

> The reality ... is that the human rights system has not succeeded in the promotion of socio-economic rights and justice in large part because political systems – political leaders and parties, as well as financial institutions – in an era of neoliberalism have not been committed to redistribution but instead have willingly facilitated the accumulation of wealth by the wealthy.[281]

What is the value of maintaining this separation between human rights and politics? Perhaps its value lies in allowing those with professional and intellectual attachments to human rights to park responsibility for any failure "in large part" in some other system. Doing so may draw the sting from critiques like Moyn's but it does nothing to make new and better futures possible. Echoing my critique (above) of Cassese's and Koskenniemi's perspectives, de Búrca's approach "shuts itself up" too much "within" human rights.[282]

To the extent that de Búrca offers proposals for a better future they involve "a wholehearted embrace of the indivisibility of civil and political rights and economic social and cultural rights" as favoured by "proponents such as Bernie Sanders and Alexandria Ocasio-Cortez."[283] If this "wholehearted embrace" fails to deliver, responsibility will, presumably, again be laid "in large part" at the door of the political system, thereby saving human rights from those, like Moyn, who can be dismissed as "advancing provocative but somewhat artificial and exaggerated critiques."[284] If it is a choice between "artificial and exaggerated critiques" that challenge human rights to directly contest material inequality, and cycles of denial driven by an apparent desire to insulate and separate human rights from the ugly realities of political contestation and global capitalism, then I choose critique.

---

280 de Búrca (n. 275) 1352.

281 Ibid.

282 "Shuts itself up" – see Adorno quotation at n. 62. "within" – see Koskenniemi quotation at n. 94, and part 2(1) of this article in general.

283 de Búrca (n. 275) 1351.

284 Ibid. 1352.

O'Connell's view offers a third, iconoclastic possibility, beyond critique and denial – namely, that attention should be focussed on "the structural character of the extant social system,"[285] which is to say, capitalism. The force of this perspective depends on its analysis of capitalism as *the* all-encompassing, global social-economic-political-legal system. On the basis outlined in part one of this article I am sympathetic to O'Connell's iconoclasm, but his argument as presented does not demonstrate why his "take-it-or-leave it" analysis should prevail over Moyn's "makeshift and ramshackle" view (and it is, of course, unrealistic to expect something on that scale from O'Connell's brief review of Moyn's book).[286] The profound and existential threats to the future and future quality of human life posed by climate change – which do not feature in Moyn's work – demonstrate why, as Kim Stanley Robinson suggests,[287] an iconoclastic, utopian perspective, akin to O'Connell's position, is essential. In the next sub-section I seek to explain why the reality of climate change tips the balance in favour of an O'Connell-type, iconoclastic perspective and against the conservative (de Búrca) and moderate (Moyn) views. For present purposes, however, I turn to consider the detail critique of Moyn's work in more detail.

O'Connell notes that *Not Enough*'s repeated "references to 'the human rights movement'" treat it "as if it were a singular monolithic entity," glossing over the divergence between the work of "large human rights multinationals" like Human Rights Watch whom Moyn critiques and the activities of smaller, more radical organisations like Via Campesina that Moyn does not discuss.[288] O'Connell's point is not that Moyn ought to have analysed all human rights organisations, but that Moyn fails to "disaggregate or unpack the complexity of 'the human rights movement.'"[289]

A concern about over-inclusiveness – about Moyn's use of intellectual drift nets that catch more than might have been intended, for all that they yield a saleable, easily packaged, easily communicated argument – also underpins de Búrca's analysis. She objects to Moyn's suggestion that "status equality,

285 See O'Connell quotation at n. 271.

286 "Take-it-or-leave it" / "makeshift and ramshackle" – see Moyn quotation at n. 279.

287 See text at n. 17 and n. 18.

288 O'Connell (n. 271). In a similar vein see Elisa Massimo (President and Chief Executive of Human Rights First), "Letter to the Editor of the New York Times," 29th April 2018, <https://www.nytimes.com/2018/04/29/opinion/human-rights.html> (last visited 2nd August 2019): "Professor Moyn's critique is based on a woefully outdated notion of who human rights activists are and what they actually do ... All over the world activists are organizing and building public support for human rights in their own societies – the Dreamers, Black Lives Matter, #MeToo, the Parkland, Fla., students and Vets for American Ideals – are gaining momentum."

289 O'Connell (n. 271).

however honoured in the breach" – 'status equality' being, in Moyn's terms, the basic idea that "[n]o one ought to be treated differently because of the kind of person they are" – "is more accepted than ever before,"[290] with a "greater consensus than ever that the high and equal status of human beings entitles them to some basic political freedoms, such as the rights to speak and to be free from torture."[291] de Búrca describes this idea of broad consensus as "breathtaking in either its naïveté or disingenuousness" in the context of inequalities in police treatment, incarceration and education affecting African-Americans, "violence against women," and widespread and persistent discrimination and violence against "'lesbian, gay, bisexual and transgender ... people of all ages and in all regions of the world'."[292] de Búrca also contests the divide Moyn maintains between "the (relatively successful [on Moyn's analysis]) struggle for status equality" and "the (unsuccessful [on Moyn's analysis]) struggle for socio-economic justice,"[293] arguing that the divide is not tenable because those "working on issues of racial equality in the USA" or "gender equality" would not see status and identity issues as "meaningfully separate" from the "socio-economic justice and material inequality" challenges facing communities and individuals.[294]

Commenting on *The Last Utopia*, Antony Anghie notes that "[i]t is a regular technique of Moyn's to acknowledge important events that might challenge his thesis and yet elide their significance for his argument."[295] Anghie suggests that Moyn has a tendency to over-simplify, noting that whilst "Moyn has an impressive ability to present complex histories and events in succinct and insightful ways ... in trying to demonstrate the distinctiveness of particular models, he may assert ... disjunctures too emphatically."[296] Anghie is concerned with particular aspects of Moyn's treatment of the history of human

---

290 Moyn, *Not Enough* (n. 228) 3.

291 Ibid.

292 de Búrca (n. 275) 1349 (quoting – "'lesbian, gay ...'" – the UN Office of the High Commissioner for Human Rights).

293 Ibid. 1350.

294 Ibid.

295 Anghie, "Whose Utopia?" (n. 261) 70.

296 Ibid. 71. Making a similar point in relation to *The Last Utopia* (n. 12) see Seyla Benhabib, "Moving beyond False Binarisms: On Samuel Moyn's The Last Utopia" (2013) 22(1) *Qui Parle* 81, 82: "I find problematic and false the philosophical binarisms Moyn sets up between morality and politics, human rights and citizens' rights, and human rights and democratic sovereignty. Some of these binarisms derive from Moyn's desire to deconstruct, in the nontechnical sense of taking apart the elements of, a certain teleological way of writing the history of human rights ... But some of his binarisms rest on his own unexamined normative assumptions."

rights but his point – that Moyn "assert[s] … disjunctures too emphatically" and diminishes the significance of evidence that speaks against his argument – maps onto de Búrca's view that Moyn draws too stark a line between status equality and material equality. Anghie seems to suggest that Moyn's arguments would not appear so "succinct and insightful" if they engaged with the true complexity of the issues they address.

Perhaps we can go one step further and contemplate the possibility that the issues Moyn chooses to address are pre-determined by his style of analysis and argumentation. Despite its focus on material equality and human well-being Moyn's utopian project does not address climate change, perhaps the most complex and insurmountable challenge to future human wellbeing and material equality. In view of Anghie's critique, it is tempting to suggest that Moyn fails to address climate change precisely because its complexity makes it an unsuitable subject for "succinct and insightful" treatment; the issue is just too complex and challenging to be addressed in a compelling, coherent and programmatic narrative.

Connecting the two central critiques on which I have focused in this section, I am suggesting that Moyn omits the *detail* of climate change from his blue-print because including that detail would disturb its coherence and appeal. Responding to climate change necessitates, I suggest, high levels of *ambition*: radical proposals capable of overhauling relations between human beings and the planet, not "moderate" proposals of the kind Moyn favours. Moyn is committed to ways of thinking that operate within the existing social and political system, and it is difficult to address climate change from that perspective. Moyn addresses that difficulty, I argue, not by reformulating his thinking to address the climate change challenge, but by excluding climate change from his thinking.

4.2 The Changing Climate

Moyn advocates global material equality without considering environmental and climatic changes that will make a good quality of life impossible to sustain for many, if not most. As Bruno Latour comments:

> Without the idea that we have [with climate change] entered into a New Climatic Regime, we cannot understand the explosion of inequalities, the scope of deregulation, the critique of globalization, or, most importantly, the panicky desire to return to the old protections of the nation-state.[297]

297 Bruno Latour, *Down to Earth* (Polity, 2018) 2.

To appreciate the significance of Moyn's failure to address climate change in a book about global equality, and in his work more generally, a brief review of global climate governance and the scale of the climate change threat is necessary.

The 2015 Paris Agreement commits (as of 2nd August 2019) 185 states to a "strengthen[ing of] the global response to the threat of climate change, in the context of sustainable development and efforts to eradicate poverty," in particular by "[h]olding the increase in the global average temperature to well below 2°C above pre-industrial levels and pursuing efforts to limit the temperature increase to 1.5°C above pre-industrial levels."[298] A 2018 IPCC (Intergovernmental Panel on Climate Change) report concluded that "[g]lobal warming is likely to reach 1.5°C between 2030 and 2052 if it continues to increase at the current rate."[299] The report also concluded that climate change commitments (in the period up to the report's publication) by Paris Agreement parties covering the period to 2030 "would not limit global warming to 1.5°C even if supplemented by very challenging increases in the scale and ambition of emissions reductions after 2030."[300]

The report details the anticipated impacts of a 1.5°C global temperature rise. "Coral reefs ... are projected to decline by a further 70–90% at 1.5°C ([the IPCC has] *high confidence* [in this conclusion])... with larger losses (>99%) at 2°C ([the IPCC has] *very high confidence* [in this conclusion]."[301] "[L]imiting global warming to 1.5°C, compared with 2°C, could reduce the number of people exposed to climate-related risks and susceptible to poverty by up to several hundred million by 2050 ([the IPCC has] *medium confidence* [in this

298 Paris Agreement, Paris, 12th December 2015, available at <https://treaties.un.org/doc/Publication/UNTS/No%20Volume/54113/Part/I-54113-0800000280458f37.pdf> (last visited 2nd August 2019), Articles 2(1), 2(1)(a). On the status of ratification of the Paris Agreement see Secretariat of the United Nations Framework Convention on Climate Change, <https://unfccc.int/process/the-paris-agreement/status-of-ratification> (last visited 2nd August 2019).

299 IPCC, 2018, "Summary for Policymakers" in Masson-Delmotte, V., P. Zhai, H.-O. Pörtner, D. Roberts, J. Skea, P.R. Shukla, A. Pirani, Moufouma-Okia, C. Péan, R. Pidcock, S. Connors, J.B.R. Matthews, Y. Chen, X. Zhou, M.I. Gomis, E. Lonnoy, Maycock, M. Tignor, and T. Waterfield (eds.), "Global Warming of 1.5°C. An IPCC Special Report on the impacts of global warming of 1.5°C above pre-industrial levels and related global greenhouse gas emission pathways, in the context of strengthening the global response to the threat of climate change, sustainable development, and efforts to eradicate poverty" (World Meteorological Organization), accessible via <https://www.ipcc.ch/sr15/chapter/spm/> (last visited 2nd August 2019), paragraph A.1.

300 Ibid., paragraph D.1.

301 Ibid., paragraph B.4.2 (italics in original).

conclusion]."[302] "[M]odel-based projections of global mean sea level rise (relative to 1986–2005) suggest an indicative range of 0.26 to 0.77 m by 2100 for 1.5°C of global warming, [which is] 0.1 m … less than for a global warming of 2°C ([the IPCC has] *medium confidence* [in this conclusion])" (and, in terms of that 0.1m difference, it is relevant to note the IPCC's related conclusion that "[a] reduction of 0.1m in global sea level rise implies that up to 10 million fewer people would be exposed to related risks, based on population in the year 2010 and assuming no adaptation ([the IPCC has] medium confidence [in this conclusion]").[303]

Kelly Levin of The World Resources Institute explains that "[t]he world is currently on track to emit more than double [the amount required to limit warming to 1.5°C] by 2030," adding that to limit warming to 1.5°C global "emissions will need to drop by 40–50 percent."[304] In summary, then, roughly four years on from the conclusion of the Paris Agreement its most ambitious target of limiting temperature increase to 1.5°C looks unachievable and, on the basis of the IPCC's 2018 report, the consequences of that appear catastrophic.

Fiji is experiencing a rise in sea level and increased sea water flooding that has "made portions of the island nation uninhabitable."[305] The vulnerability of small island developing states (SIDS) like Fiji to climate change impacts – "sea-level rise, changing precipitation patterns, increased frequency and intensity of extreme weather events, ocean acidification and coral bleaching"[306] – raises pressing issues of social and material equality. The costs and challenges of adapting to climate change place a burden on SIDS that is often met through donor aid,[307] but reliance on donor aid disempowers those directly affected by climate change: "donor funding is available for what donors see as a priority – which does not necessarily reflect communities' priorities."[308] The impact of climate change on SIDS is wholly unequitable as "[t]hey account for less than

302 Ibid., paragraph B.5.1.

303 Ibid., paragraph B.2.1.

304 Kelly Levin, World Resources Institute, "Half a Degree and a World Apart: The Difference in Climate Impacts Between 1.5°C and 2°C of Warming," 7th October 2018, <https://www.wri.org/blog/2018/10/half-degree-and-world-apart-difference-climate-impacts-between-15-c-and-2-c-warming> (last visited 2nd August 2019).

305 COP (Conference of the Parties to the United Nations Framework Convention on Climate Change) 23 website, "How Fiji is Affected by Climate Change," <https://cop23.com.fj/fiji-and-the-pacific/how-fiji-is-affected-by-climate-change/> (last visited 2nd August 2019).

306 Carola Betzold, "Adapting to climate change in small island developing states" (2015) 133(3) *Climatic Change* 481, 482.

307 See ibid., in particular at 486.

308 Ibid. 486.

1% of greenhouse gas emissions, but are among the most vulnerable to climate change impacts and sea-level rise."[309]

Germanwatch is a non-governmental climate research and policy organisation that produces an annual index analysing data "on the impacts of extreme weather events and associated socio-economic data."[310] The Germanwatch Global Climate Risk Index 2019 notes that:

> [o]f the ten most affected countries and territories (1998–2017), eight were developing countries in the low income or lower-middle income country group, one was classified as an upper-middle income country (Dominica) and one an advanced economy generating high income (Puerto Rico).[311]

The Index "indicates a level of exposure and vulnerability to extreme events, which countries should understand as warnings in order to be prepared for more frequent and/or more severe events in the future."[312] Whilst "the link between certain weather events and climate change is still a frontier in science,"[313] there is widespread support for the claim that extreme weather events and climate change are linked. The Index notes that "[t]he IPCC has already predicted that risks associated with extreme events will continue to increase as the global mean temperature rises."[314]

Extreme weather events have a real and current impact on communities and lives, predominantly in developing states. The Index notes that in 2017:

> Massive rainfalls have led to floods across Nepal, Bangladesh and India, which affected more than 40 million people. 1 200 people lost their lives in these three countries and millions were displaced throughout the region. The floods spread across the foothills of the Himalayas and brought landslides leaving tens of thousands of houses and vast areas of farmland and roads destroyed … Nearly 250 people were killed by collapsed buildings

---

309 Poh Poh Wong, "Small island developing states" (2011) 2(1) *WIREs Climate Change* 1, 2.

310 David Eckstein, Maria-Lena Hutfils and Maik Winges, "Global Climate Risk Index 2019: Who Suffers Most From Extreme Weather Events? Weather-related Loss Events in 2017 and 1998 to 2017," accessible via <https://www.germanwatch.org/sites/germanwatch.org/files/Global%20Climate%20Risk%20Index%202019_2.pdf> (last visited 2nd August 2019), 3.

311 Ibid. 4.

312 Ibid. 3–4.

313 Ibid. 10.

314 Ibid.

> or drowning in regions of India, Nepal and Bangladesh. 950 000 houses were damaged or destroyed in the floods.[315]

Moyn's *Not Enough* is sub-titled *Human Rights in an Unequal World.* The inequalities and threats to wellbeing at the heart of climate change are among the most pressing and consequential in the world today and, as the Germanwatch Index indicates, the impact of climate change is expected to intensify. Moyn has written a book about global material inequalities and pursued a wider utopian project centred on human rights and human welfare. That book and that project omit any discussion of climate change and, in particular, its acute and worsening impact on developing states in the global South. This marks Moyn's work as a product of the outdated orthodoxy that global social, economic, civil and political affairs can be debated without consideration of the environmental, reflecting a geographical bias towards the global North insofar as his work ignores the widespread, life-changing and present-day impacts of climate change on the global South. Perhaps Moyn would have written a different book had he been working at the Fiji campus of the University of the South Pacific.

A number of voices have challenged a perceived geographical bias in Moyn's work. Julieta Lemaitre, a Colombian judge, highlights what she sees as *Not Enough*'s U.S.-centrism,[316] and Karuna Mantena argues that Moyn "subsumes the NIEO [New International Economic Order] under the rubric of western welfarism, as if it were a global extension of the welfare state."[317] For Mantena Moyn emphasises the work of "Swedish economist Gunnar Myrdal" without giving the necessary prominence to "the progenitors of the NIEO themselves."[318]

Moyn notes that in 1958 Myrdal – who, in Moyn's words, "pioneered a truly global economics"[319] – "gave the Storrs lectures at Yale Law School, which took up what he cast as the defining challenge of the age: scaling up the welfare state to the world stage."[320] He also cites the view of "Dutch international lawyer B.V.A. Röling" that the NIEO "meant the universalization of principles that were already applied in the 'welfare state'" with apparent approval.[321] The

315 Ibid. 7.

316 Lemaitre (n. 263), and see Lemaitre quotations in n. 263.

317 Karuna Mantena, "Gettting the NIEO Right," 21st May 2018, *Law and Political Economy* <https://lpeblog.org/2018/05/21/getting-the-nieo-right/#more-701> (last visited 2nd August 2019).

318 Ibid.

319 Moyn, *Not Enough* (n. 228) 104.

320 Ibid. 105.

321 Ibid. 116.

prominence Moyn gives to lectures at Yale and the views of European international lawyers like Röling suggests a global North perspective, and that suggestion is strengthened by the extensive analysis of U.S-centred, 1970s global ethics scholarship in *Not Enough*'s final chapter.[322]

Not Enough lacks critical reflection on what is at stake in practices of universalisation. The argument, as presented, fails to foreground the impact of the author's own perspective on its construction. If viewed from a global South perspective it is, I suggest, inconceivable that Moyn would or could have ignored climate change. Moyn's method implies that global social reality is graspable, but "[t]he social totality is always unrepresentable."[323] "[H]umanity" is invoked on *Not Enough*'s final page but it is not clear what Moyn means by "humanity,"[324] where "humanity" lives, or whose particular interests "humanity" shares or prefers.[325] As Anghie asks, "*whose* utopia" is Moyn arguing for?[326]

Moyn protests against the charge of U.S.-centrism, arguing that whilst "[t]he book inevitably reflects some American assumptions ... it is certainly not legitimate to claim that it is about America from its revolution to the present or defiantly excludes the rest of the world in substance."[327] Maybe *Not Enough* is not "about America," and perhaps the exclusion of the "rest of the world" is not total. But it is telling that in *The Last Utopia* Moyn uses this basis to support his claim that "[t]he moral *world* had changed" in 1977:[328]

> Having been almost never used in English prior to the 1940s, when they experienced only a modest increase, the words "human rights" were

322 See ibid. chapter 6, "Global Ethics from Equality to Subsistence" (reviewing the work of John Rawls, Peter Singer, Onora O'Neill, Henru Shue and Charles Beitz).

323 Fredric Jameson, "The Utopian Enclave" in Fredric Jameson, *Archaeologies of the Future: The Desire Called Utopia and Other Science Fictions* (Verso, 2007) 10, 14.

324 Moyn, *Not Enough* (n. 228) 220: "Human rights will return to their defensible importance only as soon as humanity saves itself from its low ambitions. If it does, for the sake of global and local welfare, sufficiency and equality can again become powerful companions, both in our moral lives and in our political enterprises."

325 See Benhabib (n. 296) 90, commenting on *The Last Utopia* (n. 12): "Samuel Moyn has written a provocative book, and his warnings about the excesses of human rights euphoria need to be taken seriously. Nevertheless, these warning are based on unexamined binarisms and cannot help in the expansion of a new kind of global politics. They are written not out of a sense of solidarity with, but rather out of a tone of ironic and imperious detachment from, global human rights activism."

326 Anghie, "Whose Utopia?" (n. 261) (emphasis added).

327 Moyn, "Bias and Exclusion" (n. 290).

328 Moyn, *The Last Utopia* (n. 12) 4 (emphasis – "*world*" – added).

> printed in 1977 in the *New York Times* nearly five times as often as in any prior year in that publication's history.[329]

Moyn offers a graph that collates the use of "human rights" in the *New York Times* and the *Times* of London between 1785 and 1985.[330] On any view, that graph is evidence of the use of those terms in one U.S. and one U.K. newspaper and not, as Moyn claims, evidence of some evolving global moral consciousness (assuming, in the absence of a definition, that this is what "the moral world" is intended to signify). To suggest, as Moyn does, that a *New York Times* / the *Times* perspective is, in some sense, *the* global perspective gives – to put it mildly – the appearance of U.S.-centrism and anglophone bias.[331] Clarity and coherence are, here, achieved at the expense of detail.

Moyn includes another graph in *Not Enough*, this one "generated via Google Books Ngram Viewer" and showing "[t]he comparative prominence of [the terms] human rights and socialism, as reflected by the percentage of English-language books in which the terms appear each year."[332] The graph's two lines seem to suggest a rough correlation between a decline in the use of the term "socialism" around 1970 and, at around the same time, an increase in the use of the term "human rights." It is difficult to know how the author sees this graph – he does not say – but it suggests another false equivalence between an exclusively anglophone evidence base and global social dynamics.

These graphs of a tiny part of anglophone discourse, or the use of editorial practices at *The New York Times* as a means of capturing global social and political dynamics; Moyn's emphasis on the work of Swedish economist Myrdal and the relative downplaying of the role of NIEO leaders, both noted by Mantena,[333] alongside Moyn's focus on anglophone, 1970s global ethics scholarship;[334] his tendency to "assert ... disjunctures too emphatically" and

329 Ibid.

330 Ibid. 231 (the page is not numbered as it falls within the 'Appendixes' section of the book but comes four pages after 227).

331 See Philip Alston, "Does the Past Matter? On the Origins of Human Rights" (2013) 126 *Harvard Law Review* 2043, reviewing *The Last Utopia* (n. 12) and suggesting, at 2073, that Moyn has "an exceptionally America-centric perspective on the world," at 2070 that Moyn adopts "an excessive and unconvincing focus on the role of a handful of American international law scholars" such as Louis Henkin, and at 2049 – with reference to the *New York Times* example discussed immediately above – that Moyn's approach suffers from a "pathology ... [that] might be termed a 'search engine mentality'."

332 Moyn, *Not Enough* (n. 228) 182.

333 See text at n. 318.

334 See text at n. 322.

to "elide" counter-arguments;[335] and the omission of climate change, notwithstanding its profound significance for global justice, material equality, and any notion of the future. All of this adds up, in my view, and as Anghie seems to suggest,[336] to a scholarship whose style and clarity of argumentation is bought at the expense of rigour and depth.

The appeal of Moyn's arguments are rooted in their simplicity and clarity. *The Last Utopia* maintains that human rights achieved true global prominence in the 1970s and not in the post-war period. *Christian Human Rights* argues that in the 1930s and 1940s the Christian right established a conservative, depoliticised rights tradition that continues to dominate human rights discourse. *Not Enough* insists that human rights has done little to address material inequality and challenge neoliberalism and that future efforts must focus on this goal, reinventing human rights in essentially socialist terms. Climate change is not suited to clear, simple arguments like these. It raises questions about the historic and contemporary relationship between global North and global South, problematizing Moyn's easy invocation of a global "humanity."[337] The impacts of climate change raise questions about the sustainability of systems that societies employ to extract resources, materials, and wealth from the earth. Such questions cannot be addressed in "moderate" terms and from within the existing system because they *are* questions about the nature and viability of that system.

It is true that climate change arises from the impact on the Earth of a global human population of 7.6 billion people (on 2017 UN data) and,[338] in that sense, climate change is a global problem facing "humanity." Framing the issue in these collective terms, however, misses the vital point that responsibility for climate change is not distributed equally between all states, all individuals currently alive, or all those who have lived. States that industrialised in the early stages of the Industrial Revolution – the U.S.A., for example – bear a historic and much greater responsibility for climate change than many of the states most vulnerable to the impacts of climate change today – SIDS such as Fiji and The Federated States of Micronesia, for example – who have done, and are doing, very little to cause it.[339] States that industrialised at an early stage

335 See discussion of Anghie's critique in text at around n. 295.

336 See ibid.

337 See text above at around n. 324.

338 United Nations Department of Economic and Social Affairs, "World Population Prospects: The 2017 Revision," 21st June 2017, <https://www.un.org/development/desa/publications/world-population-prospects-the-2017-revision.html> (last visited 2nd August 2019).

339 See Maria Rocha, Mario Krapp, Johannes Guetschow, Louise Jeffery, Bill Hare, Michiel Schaeffer, "Historical Responsibility for Climate Change – from countries emissions to

acquired a global economic advantage by doing so. 'Early adopters' enjoy far greater technical, industrial and financial resources today than states which are not, in any meaningful sense, responsible for climate change despite being most exposed to its impacts (sea level rise, for example). This creates a very real divergence between states' levels of responsibility for climate change and their degree of vulnerability to it.[340]

Many states in the global North used violent and exploitative methods, including processes of international legal argumentation, to acquire and extract resources from the global South.[341] They derived economic advantage from their use of those resources and, through that use, began the process of changing the global climate. The impact of those changes is felt most acutely today by climate-vulnerable states in the global South. In a sense, then, the global North has forced the global South to bear the environmental costs associated with the economic benefit that it (the global North) derived from the forcible seizure of the global South's resources.[342] Moyn does not address this meta-level global equity issue in *Not Enough*.

---

contributions to temperature increase," November 2015, <https://climateanalytics.org/media/historical_responsibility_report_nov_2015.pdf> (last visited 2nd August 2019).

340 See Hans-Martin Füssel, "How inequitable is the global distribution of responsibility, capability, and vulnerability to climate change: A comprehensive indicator-based assessment" (2010) 20(4) *Global Environmental Change* 597, 607: "If vulnerability is interpreted narrowly as a lack of socio-economic capacity and entitlements to cope with the adverse impacts of climate change, the common assertion that those countries least responsible for climate change are most vulnerable to its impacts is clearly true," and at 607–608: "If vulnerability to climate change is interpreted more comprehensively as the expected social impacts of climate change considering current adaptive capacity, the analysis finds a double inequity between countries' responsibility / capability and vulnerability for food security, human health, and coastal populations. The equity implications of climate change for water supply are more complex ... more uncertain ... and more difficult to express by a single metric."

341 See Antony Anghie, "The Evolution of International Law: colonial and postcolonial realities" (2006) 27(5) *Third World Quarterly* 739, 745: "[Nineteenth century] [p]ositivist jurists ... devised a series of formal doctrines that used explicitly racial and cultural criteria to decree certain states civilised, and therefore sovereign, and other states uncivilised and non-sovereign. Thus non-European societies were expelled from the realm of international law. Lacking legal personality, these societies were incapable of advancing any legally cognisable objection to their dispossession, and were thus reduced to objects of conquest and exploitation."

342 See, for example, Leon Sealey-Huggins, "'1.5°C to stay alive': climate change, imperialism and justice for the Caribbean" (2017) 38(11) *Third World Quarterly* 2444, 2445: "In a perverse paradox ... wealth expropriated from the Caribbean during the period of early colonialism was expended on processes of industrialisation, which has in turn contributed significantly to the climate change-inducing emissions that now threaten Caribbean societies."

Despite the responsibility of early-industrialising states for climate change, and a sense that developed states' financial support for adaptation to the impacts of climate change in developing states would go some way to recognising that responsibility, global levels of adaptation financing fall far short of what is required. The World Resources Institute reports that "[t]hose in greatest need of assistance – communities hit first and hardest by climate change – still struggle to access funds, receive disproportionately small shares of available finance and have little say in the allocation of such scarce resources."[343]

Under President Trump the U.S. has reneged on Obama administration commitments to support the Green Climate Fund – the principal global mechanism for adaptation financing. In a June 2017 statement on U.S. withdrawal from the Paris Agreement President Trump noted that the "Green Climate Fund ... calls for developed countries to send $100 billion to developing countries all on top of America's existing and massive foreign aid payments," defending the U.S. withdrawal from the Paris Agreement on the basis that it would have required "billions of dollars that ought to be invested right here in America [to] ... be sent to the very countries that have taken our factories and our jobs away from us."[344] Trump's populist nationalism makes the result of Moyn's search for a "better compromise between utopianism and realism"[345] – *Not Enough*'s U.S.-centric call for Jacobin-esque socialism – look more like a fantastical pipedream than a realistic blueprint.

An understanding of the colonial exploitation and oppression of the global South by the global North is, for the reasons set out above, central to any understanding of industrialisation. Equally, an understanding of industrialisation (including colonial exploitation and oppression) is central to any understanding of the history of global South and global North socio-economic development. Because processes of industrialisation in large part caused climate change, and because industrialisation is embedded in the colonial exploitation and oppression of the global South, any engagement with questions of global equality is incomplete without analysis of climate change. In that sense, then, Moyn's failure to address climate change in *Not Enough* makes his entire analysis deficient. This reflects U.S.-centrism insofar as a scholar working in a more climate-vulnerable state – Fiji, for example – and

---

343 World Resources Institute, "Adaptation Finance Accountability Initiative," <https://www.wri.org/our-work/project/adaptation-finance-accountability-initiative> (last visited 2nd August 2019).

344 The White House, "Statement by President Trump on the Paris Accord," 1st June 2017 <https://www.whitehouse.gov/briefings-statements/statement-president-trump-paris-climate-accord/> (last visited 2nd August 2019).

345 See Moyn quotation at n. 230.

writing about global equality would almost certainly find it hard to ignore climate change.

The divide between climate justice and climate governance is well recognised and it would be trite – and, in the face of Trump-style populist nationalism, ineffective – to observe that the global North should do more to mitigate the impact of its present and historic economic and industrial activity on the global climate. Moyn's blueprint-style of utopianism operates by making calls of that kind, calling for socialism at a time when Trump-style self-interest and nationalism seem to be on the rise. However "succinct and insightful" Moyn's approach is,[346] and however well his books sell, arguments of that kind offer nothing new.

There is a secondary sense, beyond that concerned with climate change *per se*, in which Moyn's work and *Not Enough* in particular is out-of-step with a changing climate, the relevant climate here being the intellectual climate within utopian scholarship. There is, as we saw in the introduction to this article, a strong trend towards iconoclasm in utopian thinking, reflected in the work of scholars such as Jameson, Abensour and Marin. Moyn rejects iconoclasm, preferring blueprintism – modest correctives to orthodox histories, moderate prescriptions for a "different today."[347] He fails to address iconoclasm in any detail and John Gray critiques his work on that basis, noting "[Moyn's] partial understanding of utopianism" and insisting that "[a] project is utopian when it can be known in advance that its central objectives cannot be realized."[348]

Perhaps Moyn prefers blueprintism to iconoclasm because a plan, however outline it may be, appears more "succinct and insightful" than an extended reflection on the necessity *and* impossibility of Utopia in postmodernity.[349] Plans outlined in academic texts translate relatively easily into newspaper and magazine columns,[350] while explanations of why fundamental change is both necessary and impossible do not. I argue that Moyn's work is, in the final analysis, defined by its pursuit of aesthetic appeal to present day audiences,[351] reflecting the supremacy of commodification and consumption

346 'Succinct and insightful' – see Anghie quotation at n. 296.

347 "Different today" – see Bauman quotation at n. 26.

348 John Gray, "What Rawls Hath Wrought" (2011) 111(1) *National Interest* 81, 87.

349 "Succinct and insightful" – see Anghie quotation at n. 296.

350 See, for example, The Nation <https://www.thenation.com/authors/samuel-moyn/> (last visited 2nd August 2019); Samuel Moyn, "How the Human Rights Movement Failed," 23rd April 2018, *New York Times* <https://www.nytimes.com/2018/04/23/opinion/human-rights-movement-failed.html> (last visited 2nd August 2019).

351 See text at n. 40 and text at n. 226.

in contemporary postmodernity.[352] It seems that history today needs to be presented as "glossy images,"[353] graphs, and easily graspable narratives.

Ben Golder defends Moyn's utopianism,[354] reading *The Last Utopia* as an exercise in Foucauldian genealogy, an "historical exposure of the groundlessness and non-necessity of human rights [that] simultaneously opens the way to a reimagining of their future."[355] He maintains that Moyn's "genealogy of human rights ... teaches us to be suspicious of claims of historical necessity and progress and to work against them in the present,"[356] holding out the hope "of a different present and a possible future."[357] This, on Golder's analysis:

> is a utopianism that is reflective, self-critical and self-aware, one always attuned to the mythic and exclusionary nature of its narratives and the remainders it produces, one that never cedes possibilities to the certitudes of progress or historical reason and that, in spite (or maybe because) of knowing all that it knows of the past, never ceases to hope for a new future.[358]

Golder's defence of Moyn's blueprintism – "another, better world of dignity and respect,"[359] "a political vision of a better world in the future (but without committing himself to a classic view that it is literally impossible or unrealisable, a *ou-topos*, as [Thomas] More conceived it)"[360] – begs the question of whether a 'new' future is possible or imaginable in the contemporary present. Golder maintains that the achievement of Moyn's genealogical utopianism is to break out of "destiny" so that "the future is (better yet: *futures are*) once again thinkable."[361] Like Moyn, Golder seems to prefer blueprintism – the conviction that it is possible to imagine genuinely 'new', 'better' futures in the contemporary present – to iconoclastic utopianism. But both Golder and Moyn state their preference without seriously considering the iconoclastic alternative and

352 See text at n. 33 to n. 41.
353 See Jameson quotation at n. 41.
354 Ben Golder, "On the genealogy of human rights: an essay on ~~nostalgia~~ nostalgia" (2016) 22(2) *Australian Journal of Human Rights* 17.
355 Ibid. 24–25.
356 Ibid. 33.
357 Ibid.
358 Ibid.
359 Moyn, *The Last Utopia* (n. 12) 4, as quoted by Golder (n. 354) at 23.
360 Golder (n. 354) 23.
361 Ibid. 25.

its insistence that contemporary, postmodern conditions make the imagination of genuinely 'new' futures impossible.

5 *Cassese and Koskenniemi, Allott and Moyn*

Koskenniemi's and Cassese's engagement with utopianism is driven by their desire to stay "within" international law's boundaries. Their commitment is to international law and not to some utopian social or political project, and that precludes any possibility that, in their hands, utopianism will define international law. For Cassese and Koskenniemi blueprints for Utopia are to be found by searching through extant international law – as the contributors to Cassese's edited collection do – and not by starting with a blank sheet of paper. Philip Allott's Eutopianism is so idealistic, so much outside of international law, material reality and history, that it becomes vulnerable to the anti-utopian critiques of messianism and a tendency towards totalitarianism framed by Popper, Berlin and Arendt.[362] Having started with a blank sheet of paper Allott's project is so much his own as to be virtually no-one else's.

Moyn's project is avowedly utopian in its pursuit of a 'better' human rights system, a blueprint for action in the here and now that contrasts with Allott's ahistorical blueprint for human self-recreating through pure thought. Moyn engages with social, political and legal history far more than Allott, even if he does produce "glossy images,"[363] and, in contrast with Cassese's and Koskenniemi's approach, Moyn is not so pre-committed to the structures and practices he considers as to be entirely constrained by them. If Cassese's and Koskenniemi's approach involves unambitious inquiry into such limited utopianism as there is within international legal discourse Moyn is, by contrast, open to the possibility that utopianism might re-invent the discourse or system of human rights. Because of its grounding in social, political and legal history, and its lack of the international legal "within"-ness that defines Cassese's and Koskenniemi's work, Moyn's is the most comprehensive vision of utopianism in international legal scholarship to date.

The potential of Moyn's utopianism is, however, limited by its blueprintism. Those like O'Connell who critique Moyn for a lack of ambition maintain that his reform blueprint cannot meet contemporary social and political challenges because it accepts the basic structure of the extant social and political system. Those like de Búrca who critique Moyn's mis-directed ambition see the problem as lying elsewhere: in some other system(s) or aspect(s) of social, political and economic life. Those, like Anghie, Lemaitre, and Mantena, who insist that

362 See text at n. 202 to n. 216.

363 See text at n. 353.

every view comes from somewhere, and that no blueprint has universal application, highlight what can be seen as a parallel between Moyn's and Allott's work: the sense in which Moyn's blueprint, if implemented in places and contexts other than that from which it originates, may tend towards an oppressive violence that overrides the particular.

All these critiques bite. What Moyn offers is not *Ou-topia* (no-place), but a geographically situated, Americanised future, not *Eu-topia* (the good place) but a slightly less bad version of today.[364] This is no basis on which to plan a utopian tomorrow because this is not a valid picture of today – it lacks detail (either in general or in some specific regard), or it underestimates the importance of identity, race, and gender.[365]

Versions of these critiques could be applied to any utopian blueprint and the only way around them is to retreat to somewhere that has some limited utopian potential for a particular community. For Cassese and Koskenniemi that somewhere is the internal structure of international law with its appeal to international lawyers. For Allott that somewhere is "the cloisters of Cambridge,"[366] the utopian ideals of one's own mind, and their supposed appeal for a nebulous "humanity." Moyn's somewhere is a place made in and by his own texts, a place where the picture of the world in the *New York Times* can be presented as global, where plans to "reinstate socialism" can be made to appear credible.[367]

A somewhere to retreat to offers a (temporary) hideout from the deficiencies of any plan for a 'better' future and the impossibility of overcoming those deficiencies. The only logical alternative to retreat into some intellectual structure (international law), oneself (Allott), or text itself (Moyn), is to remain rooted in the complexity and insurmountability of contemporary reality. Doing that entails acceptance of the iconoclastic view that any plan for a better future will be deficient in ambition and / or detail and, in that sense, that the very idea of a 'plan' for a better future is impossible, for all that plans for a better future are essential: "utopia is somehow negative … it is most authentic when we cannot imagine it."[368]

The very possibility of an iconoclastic approach, grounded in the notion that answers have not been arrived at because they are not available within existing paradigms of thought and practice, requires a turn away from blueprintism. To

364 See Bauman quotation at n. 26 ("different today").
365 See text at n. 290 to n. 294.
366 See Allott quotation at n. 131.
367 "Reinstate socialism" – see Mishra quotation at n. 269.
368 Jameson, "The Politics of Utopia" (n. 7) 46 (also quoted at n. 7).

critique an iconoclastic posture on the basis that it does not have the answers is to assume that blueprints are the only form in which utopia can exist. It is also to miss the very point of the iconoclastic perspective: that moving beyond can only happen if there is recognition of the need for something beyond what is, rather than 'new' thinking within the confines of what is.

The reality of climate change concretises the need for something beyond what is. There is a gap between current commitments to reduce emissions by parties to the Paris Agreement and the scale of action necessary to limit global temperature rise to 1.5°C above pre-industrial levels.[369] If, thanks to the work of organisations such as the IPCC, we have an acutely developed understanding of the climate impact that "the consumption of sheer commodification as a process" has had and is having,[370] we have no idea of how to change that process, how to break-out of the legacies of modernity, industrialisation, and colonialism that coalesce in postmodernity.

International climate governance, in the form of the Paris Agreement, perpetuates the dream of international law as a discourse or collection of symbols or forms that offers *the* path to a better global future – indeed, the Paris Agreement seeks to define a future in which "the increase in the global average temperature [has been limited] to well below 2°C above pre-industrial levels."[371] It is time to wake up from this dream, time to cast off the notion that the Paris Agreement and other utopian blueprints like it – the Charter of the United Nations,[372] the Rome Statute of the International Criminal Court,[373] the Universal Declaration of Human Rights[374] – map the path to a truly 'better' future. Equally, it is time to reject scholarship that promotes an image of international law as a utopian blueprint, whether in limited and conservative (Cassese and Koskenniemi), moderate and pragmatic (Moyn) or totalising and idealistic (Allott) form. Contemporary international law is, at best, a "degenerate utopia" – a means of effecting "the ideological closure of the system in

369 See text at n. 304.

370 "The consumption of sheer commodification as a process" – see Jameson quotation at n. 33.

371 See text at n. 298.

372 Charter of the United Nations, San Francisco, 26th June 1945, available at <https://www.un.org/en/charter-united-nations/> (last visited 2nd August 2019).

373 Rome Statute of the International Criminal Court, Rome, 17th July 1998, 2187 UNTS 3, available at <https://www.icc-cpi.int/resource-library/Documents/RS-Eng.pdf> (last visited 2nd August 2019).

374 Universal Declaration of Human Rights, United Nations General Assembly Resolution 217A, 10th December 1948, available at <https://www.un.org/en/universal-declaration-human-rights/> (last visited 2nd August 2019).

which we are somehow trapped and confined,"[375] of sustaining the idea of the future as "a different today rather than a more felicitous tomorrow"[376] – and I turn now to that aspect of my argument.

Part 3: Utopia, "Degenerate Utopia," and Disneyland

Philosopher Louis Marin develops the concept of a "degenerate utopia" in his analysis of Disneyland (California), the original Disney theme park that first opened in 1955.[377] That theme park may seem far removed from the terrain of international law but, in what follows, I aim to show that international law is, like Disneyland, a "degenerate utopia."[378] To do that I offer an account of Marin's theory of utopia, connecting it with Fredric Jameson's Marin-informed analysis of Ursula Le Guin's and Kim Stanley Robinson's science fiction and contemporary evidence of Utopia's social and political relevance. I then consider Marin's theory of "degenerate utopia," comparing and contrasting it with his theory of utopia, to produce an account of contemporary international law as a Disneyland-esque "degenerate utopia."

1 *Neutralisation: Marin's Utopia*

For Marin Utopia is a concept of the limit, a way of thinking the attempt to move beyond what is, "the neutral name, the name of the 'neutral.'"[379] "[T]he 'netural'" – *the* key concept for Marin – "names the limit, the gap between two frontiers or two continents, the old and the new worlds."[380] Utopia "does not mean a place that is nowhere ... an island that exists only in [Thomas] More's imagination or a place that does not exist,"[381] but "designates a no-place ... *another* referent, the 'other' of any place."[382]

Utopia exists as potentiality rather than actuality. "It stands as a perfect idea above any limit,"[383] "the plural figure of the infinite work of the limit or fron-

375 See Jameson quotation at n. 7.
376 See Bauman quotation at n. 26.
377 Marin, *Utopics* (n. 4) 239.
378 Ibid.
379 Marin, "Frontiers" (n. 46) 411.
380 Ibid.
381 Ibid.
382 Ibid.
383 Ibid. 413. For an outline of a theory of international law grounded, in a sense, in the notion of "a perfect idea above any limit" see Matthew Nicholson, "Walter Benjamin and the Re-Imageination of International Law" (2016) 27 *Law and Critique* 103, in particular at 106 and 123–124.

tier or difference in history."[384] It is not to be captured in a plan or blueprint because the attempt at containment tends towards authoritarianism: "Utopia as ideology is a totality; and when political power seizes it, it becomes a totalitarian whole."[385] As Jameson, analysing Marin's work, explains:

> To understand Utopian discourse in terms of neutralization is ... to propose to grasp it as a process, as energeia, enunciation, productivity, and implicitly or explicitly to repudiate that more traditional and conventional [blueprint] view of Utopia as sheer representation, as the 'realized' vision of this or that ideal society or social ideal.[386]

Any utopian text – such as Thomas More's original *Utopia* – serves a neutralizing function.[387] More's text is not a blueprint for the construction of a future society nor a mere critique of sixteenth-century England.[388] On Marin's analysis – which Jameson endorses – it is an exercise in neutralization, "'neither anti-World, nor New World, but simply World other'":[389] "More's *Utopia* is neither England nor America, neither the Old nor the New World; it is the in-between of the contradiction at the beginning of the sixteenth century of the Old and New Worlds."[390] This is Utopia as "the third term, neither positive nor negative, of each group of categories."[391]

"Utopic practice" – the practice of writing "World other" – is "an ideological critique of the dominant ideology."[392] Ideology, here, designates *the* mode of speaking, thinking and acting, as Terry Eagleton explains:

> [T]he concept of ideology aims to disclose something of the relation between an utterance and its material conditions of possibility, when those conditions of possibility are viewed in the light of certain

384 Marin ibid.

385 Ibid.

386 Fredric Jameson, "Of Islands and Trenches: Naturalization and the Production of Utopian Discourse" (1977) 7(2) *Diacritics* 2, 6.

387 Ibid. 9: "[T]he basic relationship of the Utopian text to what we have been calling its referential sub-text is one of neutralization; or, in terms of More's *Utopia*, that the island of that name functions as a point-by-point negation or cancelling of the historical England itself" (England, here, being the "referential sub-text").

388 See quotation in n. 387.

389 Jameson, "Of Islands and Trenches" (n. 386) 11 (quoting Marin).

390 Marin, *Utopics* (n. 4) xiii.

391 Ibid.

392 Ibid. xiv.

> power-struggles central to the reproduction (or also, for some theories, contestation) of a whole form of social life.[393]

Ideology is the production of "whole form[s] of social life" through processes ("power-struggles," "material conditions of possibility") which constrain what can be said or represented ("utterance"). As Marin puts it, "ideological discourse ... expresses reality by way of a closed conceptual system whose aim is to provide a legitimizing or justificatory representation of the world."[394] Utopic practice, as "an ideological critique of the dominant ideology,"[395] seeks to neutralise a "whole form of social life" – in More's case, early sixteenth century England – by performing "World other," "subvert[ing] the picture of reality given by ideological discourse" in the process.[396]

Utopic practice is not, then, an exercise in drawing up blueprints for an alternative future.[397] It is a process of writing texts that neutralise what is, texts that "'give the signal that we are coming out of the series ... entering into the possible, the unfated ... at least into a fate that can [by reaching beyond the confines of "the dominant ideology"] be modified.'"[398] Consistent with this understanding of "Utopic practice," Fredric Jameson promotes the utopic practice of science fiction authors Ursula Le Guin and Kim Stanley Robinson.[399]

For Jameson, "Utopian space is an imaginary enclave within real social space."[400] "[R]eal social space" in postmodernity, according to Jameson, involves the bureaucratisation of life and reality by ever-more specialised disciplines, systems, and forms of knowledge.[401] Jameson evokes something of Cassese's and Koskenniemi's "within"-ness, referring to "jurists, who become a separate profession governed by a distinct field of knowledge in its own right"

393 Terry Eagleton, *Ideology: An Introduction* (Verso, 2007 [1991]), 223.

394 Louis Marin (Fredric Jameson trans.), "Theses on Ideology and Utopia" (1976) 6 *Minnesota Review* 71, 71.

395 See Marin quotation at n. 392.

396 Marin, "Theses" (n. 394) 71.

397 See ibid., 72: "[U]topia, as discourse, does not contain the method which allows it to take place, nor the methodology which would legitimate it: does not, in other words, contain the theory of its own production."

398 Marin, "Frontiers" (n. 46) 420 (quoting Ernst Bloch).

399 On Le Guin see Jameson, "The Politics of Utopia" (n. 7), 53; Fredric Jameson, "World Reduction in Le Guin" in Fredric Jameson, *Archaeologies of the Future: The Desire Called Utopia and Other Science Fictions* (Verso, 2007) 267. On Robinson see Jameson, "'If I Can Find'" (n. 24).

400 Jameson, "The Utopian Enclave" (n. 323) 15.

401 Ibid.

as an example of bureaucratised specialisation.[402] Each discipline or system carves out a distinct and sealed domain of conduct, process and behaviour for itself, fragmenting the "real social space" by doing so.[403] "Utopian space," by contrast, is a "pocket of stasis within the ferment and rushing forces of social change [that] may be thought of as a kind of enclave within which Utopian fantasy can operate."[404] Against the bureaucratisation, sub-division, and specialization of life in postmodernity, the Utopian "imaginary enclave" is "a zone of the social totality which seems eternal and unchangeable."[405]

Utopia, then, offers an image of the whole, and the "fictive" possibility of re-constructing life and reality.[406] Utopia is not concerned with the representation of "contemporary social reality" *per se* because it is "the *other* or negative of contemporary social reality [that] appears" through Utopia's "fictive construction."[407] The problem, in a sense, then, with Samuel Moyn's blueprint for human rights, or Philip Allott's Eutopian plan for international law – to take two examples from the first part of this article – is that they are presented as real(istic) and achievable when they are, in the context of postmodern, "contemporary social reality," fantastical. Moyn and Allott approach utopianism as though it is a pragmatic exercise in re-orienting thought, practice, theory, doctrine, or discourse when – as Marin's and Jameson's analysis reveals – Utopia, as a literary practice with roots stretching back to Thomas More, is a "fictive" exercise in creating "the *other* or negative" of the context in which it is written.

If we are, then, to understand the present-day value and potential of utopianism we need to consider the contemporary "fictive" literature.

2 *"Our Constitutional Inability to Imagine Utopia": Le Guin, Robinson, and Jameson*

Through analysis of Le Guin's and Robinson's works Jameson develops his thesis that "the political function of the utopian genre" and of science fiction in general "is to bring home, in local and determinate ways and with a fullness

402 Ibid.

403 See ibid. 14–15, discussing Niklas Luhmann's "systems theory," and concluding (at 15): "Luhmann defines modernity by way of the onset of this process [of specialization and stratification]; postmodernity could then be seen as a dialectical saturation in which the hitherto semi-autonomous sub-systems of these various social levels threaten to become autonomous *tout court*, and generate a very different ideological picture of complexity as dispersed multiplicity and infinite fission than the progressive one afforded by the preceding stage of modernity."

404 Ibid. 15.

405 Ibid.

406 Marin, "Theses" (n. 394) 72: "Utopia is a fictive construction."

407 Ibid. 72.

of concrete detail, our constitutional inability to imagine Utopia itself … as a result of the systemic, cultural and ideological closure of which we are all in one way or another prisoners."[408]

In *The Lathe of Heaven* Le Guin tells the story of a "hapless young man … tormented by the unwanted power to dream 'effective dreams' … which … change external reality itself … reconstruct[ing] the … historical past in such a way that the previous 'reality' disappears without a trace."[409] He seeks the help of "an ambitious psychiatrist" who harnesses this power "to change the world for the benefit of mankind."[410] The dreamer's dreams, each designed to make the world a better place, change reality again and again, with a range of unintended consequences (mass deaths and alien invasion, for example).[411]

Whilst *Lathe*'s narrative might be read "either as [a manifestation of] the liberal's anxiety in the face of a genuinely revolutionary transformation of society" – the capacity to dream a new world into being – "or as the expression of more conservative misgivings about the New Deal-type reformism and do-goodism of the welfare state,"[412] for Jameson "the deeper subject of this fascinating work can only be the dangers of imagining Utopia and more specifically of writing the utopian text itself."[413] On Jameson's analysis the book "is 'about' its own process of production."[414] Whilst the dreamer "cannot dream Utopia" into being, however much the psychiatrist wants him do so, "in the very process of exploring the contradictions of [the attempt to produce Utopia that the novel narrates], the narrative gets written, and 'Utopia' is 'produced'."[415]

The point is that Le Guin's text *is* a negative, dialectical iconoclastic Utopia because "we are shown that an 'achieved' Utopia – a full representation – is a contradiction in terms."[416] By narrating the contemporary un-dreamability of utopia Le Guin's text stages the reality of Utopia's unreality in contemporary cultural conditions. If Philip Allott was to re-visit his Eutopianism on the basis of *Lathe*, perhaps he would caveat his declaration that "[h]uman beings inhabit a *human world*, entirely made by the human mind."[417] If Samuel Moyn was to read *Lathe* into his work, perhaps he would rethink his call for human

408 Jameson, "Progress Versus Utopia" (n. 29) 289.
409 Ibid. 293; Ursula Le Guin, *The Lathe of Heaven* (Gollancz, 2001 [1971]).
410 Jameson, "Progress Versus Utopia" (n. 29) 293.
411 Le Guin, *Lathe* (n. 409).
412 Jameson, "Progress Versus Utopia" (n. 29) 293.
413 Ibid.
414 Ibid.
415 Ibid. 294.
416 Ibid.
417 See text above at n. 163.

rights to "become more scientific" by "engag[ing] in the programmatic concern with designing good states, for the sake of global economic welfare."[418]

Another of Le Guin's novels, *Left Hand of Darkness*, is set on the frozen planet of Gethen / Winter, "an inimical world; its punishment for doing things wrong is sure and prompt; death from cold or death from hunger."[419] In this "utopian enclave" a drama of gender and androgyny,[420] conflict, mediation, love and loss plays out. The two central characters are Genly Ai, a representative of the Ekumen – "a kind of galactic United Nations,"[421] "a clearing-house for trade and knowledge" that ensures "communication between the worlds of men"[422] – and Estraven, a politician in Karhide, a nation on Gethen. Genly Ai is male and Estraven, like everyone on Gethen, is androgynous. Notes prepared by Ekumen 'Investigators' – an advance party who surveyed Gethen in preparation for Genly Ai's visit – explain that the absence of gender on Gethen changes not only sex but social interaction:

> The First Mobile [Genly Ai is the 'First Mobile' or envoy from Ekumen], if one is sent, must be warned that unless he is very self-assured, or senile, his pride will suffer. A man wants his virility regarded, a woman wants her femininity appreciated, however indirect and subtle the indications of regard and appreciation. On Winter [Gethen] they will not exist. One is respected and judged only as a human being. It is an appalling experience.[423]

"Gethenian sexual physiology" involves processes of "somer" and "kemmer," somer being the non-sexually active phase of Gethenian life lasting "[f]or 21 or 22 days,"[424] and Kemmer "averag[ing] 26 to 28 days" and involving the development of sex organs:[425] "Normal individuals have no predisposition to either sexual role in kemmer; they do not know whether they will be the male or the female, and have no choice in the matter."[426]

418 See text above at n. 232 and n. 247.
419 Ursula Le Guin, *The Left Hand of Darkness* (Orbit, 1981 [1969]) 88.
420 "Utopian enclave" – Jameson, "The Utopian Enclave" (n. 323).
421 Jameson, "World Reduction" (n. 399) 280.
422 Le Guin, *The Left Hand* (n. 419) 36.
423 Ibid. 86.
424 Ibid. 82.
425 Ibid. 81.
426 Ibid. 82.

Androgynous Gethenians are "not neuters" but "potentials, or integrals."[427] The Investigator concludes "I must say 'he' [to refer to a Gethanian], for the same reasons as we used the masculine pronoun in referring to a transcendent god: it is less defined, less than the neuter or the feminine,"[428] but recognises that "the very use of the pronoun in my thoughts leads me continually to forget that the Karhider I am with is not a man, but a manwoman."[429]

Genly Ai seeks to make "an alliance with the nations of Gethen" in the interests of "[m]aterial profit. Increase of knowledge. The augmentation of the complexity and intensity of the field of intelligent life. The enrichment of harmony and the greater glory of God. Curiosity, Enrichment, Delight."[430] Just before Genly Ai's meeting with the king of Karhide Estraven is branded a traitor and banished. Karhide and Orgoreyn, another nation on Gethen, are enemies and when he travels to Orgoreyn Genly Ai is surprised to meet the newly banished Estraven. Events lead Genly Ai and Estraven to make an almost impossible journey across icy wastelands, discovering their love for each other as they travel. Out "[o]n the [i]ce" (the title of the chapter in which Genly Ai discovers his love for Estraven), having left the social and political complexities of Karhide and Orgoreyn behind, Genly Ai forgets his blueprints for intergalactic order, peace, and trade: "Estraven and I ... simply arrived at the point where we shared whatever we had worth sharing."[431] For this to happen Genly Ai has to overcome his binary understanding of gender:

> And I saw then again, and for good, what I had always been afraid to see, and had pretended not to see in him: that he was a woman as well as a man ... Until then I had rejected him, refused him his own reality.... [H]e was the only one who had entirely accepted me as a human being: who had liked me personally and given me entire personal loyalty: and who therefore had demanded of me an equal degree of recognition, of acceptance. I had not been willing to give it. I had been afraid to give it. I had not wanted to give my trust, my friendship to a man who was a woman, a woman who was a man.[432]

The Left Hand ends with the violent death of Estraven, Genly Ai's return to Karhide, and the ultimate success of his mission as an Ekumen spaceship

427 Ibid. 85.
428 Ibid.
429 Ibid.
430 Ibid. 35.
431 Ibid. 209
432 Ibid. 210.

arrives in Karhide and contact is established with the nations of Gethen. For Jameson a sense of "the Ekumen as a kind of galactic United Nations" permeates the "liberal 'solution'" of the book's conclusion.[433] Genly Ai claims, in discussions with the king of Karhide, that he and the dead Estraven served "[m]ankind" in their efforts to establish contact between Gethen and the Ekumen.[434] Privately, to the reader, however, Genly Ai notes that this was only "an aspect of the truth" for "[i]t would be no less true to say that Estraven's acts had arisen out of pure personal loyalty" to him.[435]

Genly Ai admits that he summoned the Ekumen spaceship that is on its way as he meets with the king "[t]o force [the king's] hand," invoking his "duty towards Gethen and the Ekumen" as justification.[436] This sense of knowing better – of gently *and* forcibly bringing about socialisation between Karhide and the Ekumen – has overtones of the colonial "civilising mission."[437] For an international legal readership *The Left Hand* might evoke memories of de Vitoria's *On the Indians Lately Discovered*, a sixteenth century text on the legal aspect of Spanish conquests in the 'new world.'[438] According to Antony Anghie:

> Vitoria argues that all peoples, including the Indians, were governed by a basic "natural law." While others characterised the Indians as heathens, and animals, lacking any cognisable rights, Vitoria instead humanely asserts of the Indians that "the true state of the case is that they are not of unsound mind, but have according to their kind, the use of reason ..." [I]t is precisely because they possess reason that the Indians are bound by a universal natural law.[439]

On this basis Anghie maintains that the people of the New World, held to the standards of European natural law, would "by their very existence and their own unique identity and cultural practices, violate this law."[440] Vitoria, Anghie

433 Jameson, "World Reduction" (n. 399) 280.

434 Le Guin, *The Left Hand* (n. 419) 246.

435 Ibid. 246–247.

436 Ibid. 247.

437 On the history and continuing relevance of the "civilising mission" in international law see Ralph Wilde, *International Territorial Administration: How Trusteeship and the Civilizing Mission Never Went* Away (Oxford University Press, 2008).

438 See Francisci de Victoria (Ernest Nys ed.), *De Indis et De ivre belli relectiones being parts of Reflectiones Theologicae XII* (The Carnegie Institution of Washington, 1917). As Anghie, "The Evolution of International Law" (n. 341) 752 (endnote 7) notes, "Victoria is more usually referred to as 'Vitoria'."

439 Anghie, "The Evolution of International Law" (n. 341) 742–743 (quoting Vitoria).

440 Ibid. 743.

argues, maintained that the Spanish had a right to travel to and trade with the New World, and that "any Indian resistance to Spanish incursions would amount to an act of aggression by the Indians that justified the Spanish in using force in self-defence – and, in doing so, in endlessly expanding their territory, conquering the native rulers in the process."[441] What starts with contact, trade and universality – with "mankind," communication, trade and knowledge – ends with wars for control of the New World, with the landing of spaceships.

According to Jameson, "the deepest subject of [*The Left Hand*] ... would not be utopia as such, but rather our own incapacity to conceive it in the first place."[442] In reaching this view he attaches particular importance to this line from a chapter 'written' by Estraven:[443] "To learn which questions are unanswerable, and *not to answer them*: this skill is most needful in times of stress and darkness."[444] This sense of remaining neutral recurs elsewhere in the chapter. Estraven tells the reader that "[t]o oppose something is to maintain it,"[445] that "[t]o be an atheist is to maintain God."[446] We need new ways of doing things, not mere opposition to what is. We need something other than one of the two options constructed by the binary-ness of existing debates:

> To oppose vulgarity is inevitably to be vulgar. You must go somewhere else; you must have another goal; then you walk a different road ... Orgoreyn and Karhide both must stop following the road they're on, in either direction; they must go somewhere else, and break the circle.[447]

The challenge of "break[ing] the circle" permeates *The Left Hand*, for all that Genly Ai's resolution of the narrative *via* the arrival of a spaceship involves a closure of, rather than a break in, the circle. That closure takes the form of the arrival of the Ekumen, and the initiation of a process through which, as Genly Ai tells the king of Karhide, "you [the people of Gethen] find unity."[448] The desire for a break, "the desire called utopia,"[449] permeates the book but – of course – it goes unrealised and, in that sense, Estraven, as the voice of utopian

441 Ibid.

442 Jameson, "World Reduction" (n. 399) 280.

443 Ibid. 279.

444 Le Guin, *The Left Hand* (n. 419) 132 (emphasis in original).

445 Ibid.

446 Ibid.

447 Ibid. 132, quoted in part by Jameson, "World Reduction" (n. 399) 279.

448 Le Guin, *The Left Hand* (n. 419) 246.

449 See Fredric Jameson, *Archaeologies of the Future: The Desire Called Utopia and Other Science Fictions* (Verso, 2007) ix (title page of part one of the book).

desire – the narrative personification not of Utopia *per se* but of the desire for it – had to die.

The book ends with Estraven's son taking on his parent's role as the voice of utopian desire, asking Genly Ai "[w]ill you tell us about the other worlds out among the stars – the other kinds of men, the other lives?"[450] The child asks to be told stories about the 'other,' perhaps in the hope that through such stories we, as readers, might learn to "break the circle." Le Guin spends more than two hundred pages telling a story of the 'other,' of Gethen, offering a non-answer to the "unanswerable" question of how in this time of "stress and darkness" we might imagine a Utopian 'other.'[451] Fittingly, the book ends with a child's request for more such stories, a request that seems to break down the wall between writer and reader, effecting something like an *Umfunktionierung*.[452]

As with *Lathe of Heaven*, in and through Le Guin's text "'Utopia' is 'produced'" by a staging of the dialectical impossibility of / imperative for Utopia in contemporary human reality,[453] transposed from Earth to the "utopian enclave" of Gethen.[454] A dialectical sensibility infuses the whole book, expressed most clearly in lines invoking the book's title: "Light is the left hand of darkness, and darkness the right hand of light. Two are one, life and death, lying together like lovers in kemmer, like hands joined together, like the end and the way."[455] On Gethen the "circle" of gender is broken and neutralised in androgyny but, as the child's question at the end of the book demonstrates, a wider, more complete breaking of the circle that defines contemporary social, political and economic reality is not achieved.

Le Guin's staging of Utopia as an impossibility / imperative in *Lathe* and *The Left Hand* can be read together and in harmony with Theodor Adorno's seminal work of critical philosophy, *Negative Dialectics*, published in 1966 (*The Left Hand* was published in 1969, *Lathe* was published in 1971). Adorno, like Estraven, opposes binary choices within the limits of existing options because "[w]hat is must be changeable if it is not to be all,"[456] because "the conceptual totality is mere appearance."[457] In terms that seem to speak to Genly Ai's initial rejection of androgyny on Gethen, and his attempt to bring Gethen into a unified Ekumen, Adorno observes that "[w]hat we differentiate will appear

450 Le Guin, *The Left Hand* (n. 419) 253.
451 "Unanswerable," "stress and darkness" – see Le Guin quotation at n. 444.
452 On "Umfunktioniering" see text at n. 190 to n. 196.
453 "'Utopia' is 'produced'" – see Jameson quotation at n. 415.
454 "Utopian enclave" – Jameson, "The Utopian Enclave" (n. 323).
455 Le Guin, *The Left Hand* (n. 419) 199.
456 Adorno, *Negative Dialectics* (n. 62) 398.
457 Ibid. 5.

divergent, dissonant, negative for just as long as the structure of our consciousness obliges it to strive for unity: as long as its demand for totality will be its measure for whatever is not identical with it."[458]

Against the maintenance or defence of what is, Adorno insists that the focus must be on what lies beyond the extant totality: "An order that shuts itself up in its own meaning will shut itself away from the possibility above order";[459] "[t]he whole is the false;"[460] "[t]rue thought is thought that has no wish to insist on being in the right."[461]

An attempt to reach for something 'other' underpins Kim Stanley Robinson's *Mars* trilogy. The "conditions of Being" are transformed in Robinson's dramatization of the human colonisation of Mars *via* terraforming, "the process of creating an Earth-like or habitable environment on another planet."[462] For Jameson, Robinson's narrative sits on "the fault line between realism and something else, which [Jameson] ... call[s] ontology."[463] Whilst there are realist elements in Robinson's narrative – extensive detail on the science of terraforming,[464] an "inventory" of the "variety of tools and materials" required[465] – to describe this as realist literature is, for Jameson, to miss its true significance:

> "Terraforming" ... retroactively includes all those implements, all those receptacles of human value [tools, materials, science, data, facts], and it becomes the fundamental dividing line between realism as the narrative of human praxis and ontology as the traces of Being itself: two formal or generic possibilities, which thereby reinforce each other, insofar as production requires some pre-existent being on which to do its work, while Being itself can be detected only in the spaces that human praxis spares, in the evanescent chance at origins that time and history inexorably efface.[466]

The Mars trilogy dramatizes the (fictive) science and politics of terraforming and the Being created *and* destroyed by terraforming: "[T]he hard SF content

458 Ibid. 5–6.

459 Ibid. 397 (also quoted at n. 62 and n. 95).

460 Theodor Adorno, *Minima Moralia: Reflections from Damaged Life* (Verso, 2005 [1951]) 50.

461 Theodor Adorno and Max Horkheimer, *Towards a New Manifesto* (Verso 2011) 71.

462 NASA, "Mars Terraforming Not Possible Using Present-Day Technology," 30th July 2018, <https://www.nasa.gov/press-release/goddard/2018/mars-terraforming> (last visited 2nd August 2019).

463 Jameson, "If I Can Find" (n. 24) 402.

464 Ibid. 393–394.

465 Ibid. 403.

466 Ibid.

[the 'science'] stands revealed as socio-political – that is to say, as utopian."[467] The point, here, is that the Earthly, familiar divide between science and politics falls away as Martian colonisers grapple with questions about what can and what should be done on and to this 'new' planet.

A drama of ecological, planetary politics plays out across the trilogy and its relevance for Earth is staged through "the obligatory return tourist trip to Earth itself."[468] During that trip one of the central characters "address[es] ... the Terran [i.e. Earth-based] welcomers,"[469] telling them:

> The move to Mars was a purifying voyage, stripping away all but the most important things. What happened in the end was Terran through and through ... we can most help the home planet by serving as a way for you to see yourselves. As a way to map out an unimaginable immensity.[470]

In this way Robinson's text "inscribe[s] the structural condition of [its] possibility within the narrative itself."[471] Robinson's trilogy does not "dramatize a single utopian possibility" but is "'polymorphic' ... [in its] inclu[sion] of the struggle between a whole range of utopian alternatives, about which it deliberately fails to conclude."[472] From this, Jameson extracts these lessons:

> The utopian text is not supposed to produce th[e] synthesis [, the solution,] all by itself or to represent it; that is a matter for human history and for collective praxis. It is supposed only to produce the requirement of the synthesis, to open the space into which it is to be imagined.[473]

> [U]topia as a form is not the representation of radical alternatives; it is rather simply the imperative to imagine them.[474]

It is of course possible to dismiss Le Guin's and Robinson's work as mere fiction, just as the word 'Utopia' can be used to dismiss ambitions for something other than what is. Such responses miss the point of the "fictive,"[475] the utopian, and

467 Ibid. 396.
468 Ibid. 410.
469 Ibid. 411.
470 Ibid. (quoting Robinson).
471 Ibid. 403.
472 Ibid. 410.
473 Ibid. 409.
474 Ibid. 416 (also quoted at n. 24).
475 "Fictive" – see text at / Marin quotation in n. 406.

the 'other' however. Jameson's analysis of Le Guin's and Robinson's work, and that work in its own right, posits the necessity of something that synthesizes discordant elements of contemporary reality into something other than what is.

To gain some sense of the contemporary necessity of a new "synthesis," inquiry into discordant elements in contemporary society, into whatever evidence there might be of the existence of a desire to "break the circle," is necessary.

3 *Finding the Exit: Brexit, Theranos, Fyre, Bolsanaro …*

Some readings of the contemporary social and political situation suggest that the utopian "imperative" is only too well understood,[476] that there is a real "desire called utopia,"[477] and that the absence of a systemic alternative to what is makes that desire stronger.

William Davies, writing in February 2019, interprets the UK's decision to leave the European Union – 'Brexit' – as the manifestation of "a deep, generalised urge to depart" in "British political culture,"[478] in a way that seems to exemplify the disconnect between utopian desire and the realisation of utopian blueprints. Davies presents Brexit as an exercise in "the ideology – or the fantasy – of exit" from consumer markets.[479] In theory, if a consumer is dissatisfied with a product or service they "exit" by withdrawing their custom, but "markets never quite match up to this ideal" because people rarely "exit" in this way, preferring instead to "make a fuss."[480] On Davies' reading Brexit "isn't so much a celebration of sovereignty or democracy, as a new frontier in the marketisation of politics" driven by the illusion of the consumer's "exit" sanction.[481] Nothing, for Davies, shows the consumer logic of Brexit better than the Brexiteer mantra that "you don't get a good deal on anything unless you're willing to walk away."[482] It is, then, one thing to want to leave the European Union and an altogether 'other' (i.e. other worldly) thing to realise that desire.

Brexit is not the only contemporary example of a utopian desire for something beyond what is *and* the impossibility of translating that desire into a blueprint. Take, as another example, the recent revelations about US biotech firm Theranos and its founder Elizabeth Holmes.[483] By revolutionising medical

---

476 See Jameson quotation at n. 474.
477 Jameson, *Archaeologies* (n. 449) ix (title page of part one of the book).
478 William Davies, "Leave, and Leave Again" (2019) 41(3) *London Review of Books* 9, 9.
479 Ibid.
480 Ibid.
481 Ibid.
482 Ibid.
483 Deborah Friedell, "A chemistry is performed" (2019) 41(3) *London Review of Books* 33.

testing with their blood testing device Theranos offered "accurate results from just a few drops of blood ... us[ing] the same blood sample to test for hundreds of different conditions simultaneously."[484] Holmes promised "'[a] world in which no one ever has to say goodbye too soon,'"[485] a Utopia in which people can buy control over their medical future.

The Theranos story was not true:

> [T]he company had been running most of its blood samples through the standard large commercial analysers made by the German conglomerate Siemens. Theranos had to dilute their tiny samples so that they could run through the machines ... [and] the results couldn't be trusted. Holmes's device, the Edison, could only run a few tests, and its "results were no better than guesswork." When employees ran their own blood through it, 20 per cent of them tested positive for syphilis.... When she sought investors, [Holmes] avoided the biotech venture capital firms that would have demanded due diligence in favour of the charmable global rich.[486]

Theranos' Utopia was sustained by the widely held desire for what Holmes was selling. Rupert Murdoch, the family behind Walmart, and Betsy DeVos (current US secretary of education) invested.[487] In 2014 *Fortune* magazine published a hagiographic article about Theranos and Holmes, extolling the efficiency and affordability of Theranos's testing methods.[488] When the truth about Theranos began to come out in 2015, after a pathologist in Missouri called a journalist at the *Wall Street Journal* because he did not believe the Theranos story could be true,[489] the *Fortune* journalist who wrote the 2014 article published "a protracted correction:"[490] "As much as I'd like to say that Holmes lied to me, I don't think she did. I do believe I was misled – intentionally – but I was also culpable, in that I failed to probe certain exasperatingly opaque answers that I repeatedly received."[491] US supermarket Walgreens allowed Theranos to set up shop

484 Ibid.

485 Ibid.

486 Ibid. 34 (paragraph breaks suppressed).

487 Ibid. 33.

488 Roger Parloff, "This CEO is out for blood" *Fortune*, 12th June 2014 <http://fortune.com/2014/06/12/theranos-blood-holmes/> (last visited 2nd August 2019).

489 Friedell (n. 483) 34.

490 Parloff, "This CEO" (n. 488) – see the note at the top of the article: "Author's note: On December 17, 2015, I published a protracted correction to this article."

491 Roger Parloff, "How Theranos Misled Me" *Fortune*, 17th December 2015 <http://fortune.com/2015/12/17/how-theranos-misled-me-elizabeth-holmes/> (last visited 2nd August 2019).

in a number of their stores, as did their rival Safeway:[492] "Walgreens executives had feared that if they hesitated to go into partnership with Theranos, they would lose out to their rivals."[493] Utopia seems to sell – to supermarkets, to journalists, to "the charmable global rich" – but everybody buying it pays to forget that Utopia is, in one of its senses, 'no-place.'

The story of 2017's Fyre festival seems to transplant the essence of the Theranos story into an entertainment and tourism setting. The plan, developed by entrepreneur Billy McFarland and rapper Ja Rule, was to hold a luxury music festival on a private island in the Bahamas.[494] The plan failed, the festival was cancelled, festival-goers were temporarily stranded in the Bahamas,[495] McFarland has been jailed for fraud,[496] and festival goers are suing the organisers.[497] Fyre was announced online in a video that opens with a voiceover insisting "all these things that may seem big and impossible are not," featuring "supermodels," jet skis, beaches, crashing waves, and a deep-blue ocean.[498] The imagery and the sales pitch involve an exit from the norm, a departure from what is through travel to a private island:[499] Thomas More's *Utopia* for Millennials.

Fyre invoked a sense of transgression, of pushing back against the orthodox – the island venue was, according to the promotional video's text, "once owned by [drug baron] Pablo Escobar."[500] Social media 'influencers' were paid to promote Fyre on Instagram – Kendall Jenner was reportedly paid $250,000 for one

492 Friedell (n. 483) 33.

493 Ibid. 34.

494 See Joe Coscarelli and Melna Ryzik, "Fyre Festival, a Luxury Music Weekend, Crumbles in the Bahamas" *New York Times*, 28th April 2017 <https://www.nytimes.com/2017/04/28/arts/music/fyre-festival-ja-rule-bahamas.html> (last visited 2nd August 2019).

495 Ibid.

496 The Guardian, "Fyre festival: creator of disastrous event sentenced on fraud charges," 11th October 2018, <https://www.theguardian.com/us-news/2018/oct/11/fyre-festival-billy-mcfarland-sentenced-prison-fraud> (last visited 2nd August 2019).

497 See Leigh Blickley, "'Hell Has No Wrath Like a Millennial Scorned': Lawyer Suing Fyre Festival Gives Updates on Case" *Huffington Post*, 17th January 2019, <https://www.huffingtonpost.co.uk/entry/fyre-festival-documentaries-laywer_us_5c3e5d70e4b0922a21d9984d?ec_carp=7365817290276570262&guccounter=1> (last visited 2nd August 2019).

498 See Fyre Festival, "Announcing Fyre Festival" <https://www.youtube.com/watch?v=mz5kY3RsmKo> (last visited 2nd August 2019).

499 See Hunter Harris, "Fyre Festival Was Terrible Before it Even Began" *Vulture*, 5th May 2017 <https://www.vulture.com/2017/05/fyre-festival-fiasco-the-complete-timeline.html> (last visited 2nd August 2019), outlining a timeline of Fyre Festival's development and failure.

500 Fyre Festival, "Announcing Fyre Festival" (n. 498).

post.[501] Fyre's 'good' place – "supermodels," the best of everything, a private, luxury island – existed only in social media's no place, and even there Fyre was a meaningless orange tile tweeted, and re-tweeted, and re-tweeted: "'A couple of powerful models posting an orange tile is what essentially built this entire festival' … says Mick Purzycki, one of the men behind Fyre Festival, in a new Netflix documentary."[502] The non-existence and impossibility of this festival was Fyre's 'unique selling point.' '"Fyre was basically like Instagram coming to life"' says DJ Jillionaire in the Fyre Netflix documentary,[503] his hyperbolically exaggerated name only too appropriate for this non-event.

Heightening the parallel with Thomas More's *Utopia*, the venue featured in the marketing material for Fyre was not the actual festival venue. McFarland and his associates forfeited the lease on the intended island venue after violating its terms – the lease prohibited any mention of Pablo Escobar but they mentioned the name in marketing material anyway – and had to relocate to a patch of land on a neighbouring island.[504] Nothing about this Instagram Utopia is certain or fixed. Two competing documentary films, one made by Netflix, the other by Hulu, offer competing narratives about culpability for the festival's failure amid claims that the festival's marketing firm exerted too much influence over the Netflix film.[505] Fyre's exit from what is turned out to be non-existent, and nobody can agree why. This is Utopia as negation, as neutralisation; as a representation of the contemporary impossibility of exiting or escaping from what is even when you have the money for the ticket.

Much of contemporary politics seems, like Brexit, to be driven by the desire for something 'other,' by a search for an exit from what is. In 2018 Brazil elected Jair Bolsanaro as its president. Offering something like an alternative to Brazil's recent history of corruption and political intrigue,[506] Bolsanaro's political career involves flirtation with an end to the liberal democratic

---

501 See Harris (n 499).

502 Olivia Ovenden, "Fyre Festival Was An Even Bigger Shitshow Than We Thought" *Esquire*, <https://www.esquire.com/uk/culture/a25854517/fyre-festival-was-an-even-bigger-shitshow-than-we-thought/> (last visited 2nd August 2019).

503 Zoe Kleinman, "Has Fyre Festival burned influencers?" *BBC News*, 22nd January 2019 <https://www.bbc.co.uk/news/46945662> (last visited 2nd August 2019).

504 See the Netflix documentary, "Fyre: The Greatest Party that Never Happened," <https://www.netflix.com/gb/title/81035279> (last visited 2nd August 2019).

505 See Josephine Livingstone, "Fyre Festival Was a Huge Scam. Is Netflix's Fyre Documentary a Scam, Too?" *The New Republic*, 12th February 2019 <https://newrepublic.com/article/153095/fyre-festival-huge-scam-netflixs-fyre-documentary-scam-too> (last visited 2nd August 2019).

506 On that recent history see Perry Anderson, "Bolsanaro's Brazil" (2019) 41(3) *London Review of Books* 11.

orthodoxy *via* "military dictatorship ... the death penalty ... easier access to guns ... [and attacks on] leftists, homosexuals and other [perceived] enemies of society."[507] Brazil seems to prefer (perceived) authoritarian order, personified by a Twitter-campaigning strongman, to the continuing complexity and incoherence of democratic politics.[508] This might seem more Dystopia than Utopia but it is worth remembering, as Juliette Werlin points out, that in More's original text "rules operate seamlessly, with a uniform predictability that extends across every inch of territory and to every citizen living within its borders" within a rigid order of "[n]umbers:"[509]

> The 54 cities of Utopia each contain 6,000 households, governed by 200 lower magistrates who are themselves supervised by 20 higher officials. Utopian citizens adhere to a fixed schedule: "dividing the day into twenty-four hours, appoint six of these for work, three of which are before dinner and three after; they then sup, and at eight o'clock counting from non, go to bed and sleep eight hours." Outside the cities, utopians serve rotating two-year shifts working on farms, where they live in households of at least 40 men and women, plus two slaves.[510]

Utopia as a highly structured, authoritarian society where order matters more than equality (noting the reference to "slaves") – perhaps Bolsanaro would approve.

Turkey, under Recep Tayyip Erdoğan, is widely regarded as an authoritarian state. Ella George tells a tale of exit, after exit, after exit in recent Turkish history, interpreting Erdoğan's agenda as a "counter-revolution,"[511] an exercise in "setting the clock back not to the moment of the republic's founding [in 1923] but a century earlier, before the modernising and Westernising reforms of the 19th century."[512] According to George, Erdoğan has a "fascination with the Ottomans" and with "Abdul Hamid II, the last sultan who had real control over the Ottoman Empire" in particular.[513] Whilst Erdoğan apparently regards Hamid as "a far-sighted reformer who would have modernised the state in ways

507 Ibid. 19.

508 See Anderson (n. 506).

509 Juliette Werlin, "Nowhere Now: Thomas More's 'Utopia' at 500" *Los Angeles Review of Books*, <https://lareviewofbooks.org/article/nowhere-now-thomas-mores-utopia-at-500/> (last visited 2nd August 2019).

510 Ibid.

511 Ella George, "Purges and Paranoia" (2018) 40(10) *London Review of Books* 22, 22.

512 Ibid.

513 Ibid. 32.

consistent with indigenous Turkish traditions had he not been undermined by a Westernising clique,"[514] for George "Erdoğan's Hamidian myths sanitise history" because:[515]

> Hamid was responsible for a period of unprecedented repression, suspending the constitution and dissolving parliament ... establish[ing] a network of informants and adopt[ing] a paranoid style of government that made him deeply unpopular ... [in a] dark chapter of Ottoman history, known as the *istibdat* ("tyranny") period.[516]

First comes an exit from the Ottoman period with the formation of the secular Republic in 1923.[517] After a few false starts, as challenges to Turkey's secularism were repressed in the late-1990s, comes the rise of the AKP – Erdoğan's political party – in the early 2000s and an attempt at Turkey's re-Ottomanisation.[518] George's account ends with the suggestion that opposition to Erdoğan is on the rise,[519] the negativity of anti-Erdoğanism seemingly overriding any sense of a positive next step. Flawed attempts to satisfy desires *via* blueprints generate disaffection, which leads to calls for an exit, which forms into a blueprint that fails to satisfy the exit-desire out of which it arose, which, in turn, inspires a desire for an exit from the most recent blueprint ...

The now-ness of a pervasive "desire called utopia,"[520] of a groundswell of support "for exiting the series,"[521] is easily narrated. Take the Utopian negativity of Brexit and add one false revolution in medical testing (Theranos), a sprinkling of flawed attempt to create an island 'paradise' for millennials (Fyre), widespread public support for *and* opposition to the authoritarian pursuit of 'order', 'stability' and 'progress' (Bolsanaro, Erdoğan) and you have a sense (and only a sense) of contemporary negativity, of now's utopian anti-ness. This is a narrative – the global, collective truth is not available, not representable.[522] As

514 Ibid.
515 Ibid.
516 Ibid.
517 See ibid. at 22.
518 See ibid. at 23 and generally.
519 See ibid. at 32.
520 Jameson, *Archaeologies* (n. 449) ix (title page of part one of the book).
521 "For exiting the series" – see Marin quotation at n. 20.
522 See Fredric Jameson, "War and Representation" in Fredric Jameson, *The Antinomies of Realism* (Verso, 2013) 232, 257: "The language of the existential individual already possesses an elaborate history with all kinds of stereotypes that it can be the task of representation to correct, disrupt, undermine or metaphysically challenge. That of the collective does

a narrative this account self-consciously admits its failure to represent the lives, realities, and experiences of billions of people it unforgivably, yet unavoidably, fails to engage with. That does not make this narrative a mere fiction (which does not, of course, mean that it is a 'fact'), just as Le Guin's and Robinson's science fiction is "fictive" without being mere fiction.[523]

Contemporary Utopian possibility lies in the attempt to maintain negativity and anti-ness, to move into and stay in a space or moment that calls for the creation of something else, something 'next,' even though its form and content are unimaginable. Despite their failure, hopelessness, and deceptiveness, in their sheet anti-ness Brexit, Theranos, Fyre, Bolsanaro's Brazil and Erdoğan's Turkey manifest a negative, iconoclastic utopianism. International law rejects such utopianism, preferring to neutralise attempts to neutralise what is by staying within its / the existing form(s), and it is in this sense that international law is a "degenerate utopia."

4 *International Law and Louis Marin's "Degenerate Utopia"*

If Utopia is "the name of the 'neutral,'"[524] and if "utopic practice ...[is] an ideological critique of the dominant ideology,"[525] then "a degenerate utopia is ideology changed into the form of a myth."[526]

A "degenerate utopia" counteracts the neutralising efforts of utopic practice by stabilising ideology in fixed, mythical form. International law, as an "ideological discourse,"[527] is "a closed conceptual system" – treaties, state practice, *opinio juris*, *jus cogens*, obligations *erga omnes*, concepts of territory, statehood,

not yet exist. Group, nation, clan, class, general will, multitude – all these remain so many linguistic experiments for designating an impossible collective totality, a manifold of consciousnesses as unimaginable as it is real."

523 "Fictive" – see text at n. 406 to n. 407 / Marin quotation in n. 406. See Fredric Jameson, "The Historical Novel Today, Or, Is It Still Possible?" in Fredric Jameson, *The Antinomies of Realism* (Verso, 2013) 259, at 298: "[T]he historical novel of the future (which is to say of our own present) will necessarily be Science-Fictional inasmuch as it will have to include questions about the fate of our social system, which has become a second nature." See also Fredric Jameson, "Coda: Kluge, or, Realism After Affect" in Fredric Jameson, *The Antinomies of Realism* (Verso, 2013) 187, at 189, noting "the impending crisis of the fictional" with reference to Thomas Mann's *Doktor Faustus*, this line having particular significance: "'Only the non-fictional is still permissible, the unplayed, the undisguised and untransfigured expression of suffering in its actual moment'." And see ibid. at 190: "[T]he weakening of the fictional also tends to undermine its opposite number, the category of the factual."

524 Marin, "Frontiers" (n. 46) 411.

525 Marin, *Utopics* (n. 4), xiv.

526 Ibid. 239.

527 Marin,"Theses" (n. 394) 71.

jurisdiction – "[that] provid[es] a legitimizing ... justificatory representation of the world."[528] This is an image of legal texts, norms, institutions and processes as guarantors of order and harmony, as effective means of controlling and stabilising lives, realities, and events.

Under the banner of a "culture of formalism" Martti Koskenniemi's work on international legal history and theory amounts to an "ideological discourse"-type understanding of international law.[529] Formalism's value, according to Koskenniemi, lies in its openness, its status as "a practice that builds on formal arguments that are available to all under conditions of equality."[530] Koskenniemi's "culture of formalism" serves as a code of professional ethics, expressing the conviction that:

> when professional men and women engage in an argument about what is lawful and what is not, they are engaged in a politics that imagines the possibility of a community overriding particular alliances and preferences and allowing a meaningful distinction between lawful constraint and the application of naked power.[531]

At its core, formalism means that "'whether we like it or not, law is based on words, words formulated in statutes, in treaties, in conventions, in customary law.'"[532] Those "words" create the structure within which legal practice operates, generating a sense of international law as a practice of "being 'within'."[533] Koskenniemi's approach seeks to discover qualifiedly utopian possibilities within the existing international legal structure:[534]

> Formalism's utopian moment lies in its resistance towards being reduced to structure (which is anyway indeterminate) or pure subjectivity ([Carl] Schmitt's "decision"), and in its identifying itself as a practice of decision-making that persists in time and through which the aspirations

528 Ibid.

529 Martti Koskenniemi, *The Gentle Civilizer of Nations: The Rise and Fall of International Law 1870–1960* (Cambridge University Press, 2001) – see 494–509 on the "culture of formalism." For my thoughts on Koskenniemi's *oeuvre* more generally see Nicholson, "Psychoanalyzing" (n. 81).

530 Koskenniemi ibid. 501.

531 Ibid. 502.

532 Ibid. 498 (quoting Wolfgang Friedmann).

533 See the title of part 2(1) of this article, and Koskenniemi quotation ("within") at n. 94.

534 See text at n. 83 and n. 85.

> of self-determining communities remain alive – even as (or perhaps precisely because) the universal they embody remains only a "horizon."[535]

Whilst formalism may have some measure of "resistance" to "structure" it remains fundamentally structural; there is no form without structure, without *the* "words." Indeterminacies in international law's structure make international law "a practice of decision-making," and there are opportunities for "critique and contestation" within the gaps in the structure,[536] but the structure fixes the scope of any decision and the limits of critique. There is nothing utopian, in Marin's and Jameson's sense, in this position. Implicitly opposing iconoclastic efforts to neutralise, negate, and write "World other," Koskenniemi understands Utopia as a limited opportunity for legal-professional creativity within what is, in the same way that visitors to Disneyland can only discover "Disney's utopia":

> Disney's utopia really is not a utopia.... [T]he visitors to Disneyland are put in the place of the ceremonial storyteller. They recite the mythic narrative of the antagonistic origins of society. Their path through the park is the narrative, recounted umpteen times, of the deceptive harmonization of contrary elements, of the fictional solution to conflicting tensions. By "acting out" Disney's utopia, the visitor "realizes" the ideology of America's dominant groups as the mythic founding narrative of their own society.[537]

Eugene D. Hill, commenting on Marin's Disneyland analysis, observes that "Disneyland ... [is] immobiliz[ed] in ideology ... function[ing] more like a myth: it papers over the contradictions instead of allowing them to 'play'."[538] On Marin's analysis, play, movement, and the absence of fixity or form are central to Utopia.[539] In international law the scope for such play and movement are heavily constrained by structures of "words," making international law a structured, ordered space of stabilisation, rather than a utopian space of neutralisation, negation and possibility.

535 Koskenniemi, *Gentle Civilizer* (n. 529) 508 (citing Ernesto Laclau).

536 "Critique and contestation" – see Koskenniemi quotation at n. 78.

537 Marin, *Utopics* (n. 4) 240–241.

538 Eugene D. Hill, "The Place of the Future: Louis Marin and His 'Utopiques'" (1982) 9(2) *Science Fiction Studies* 167, 176.

539 Marin, *Utopics* (n. 4) 246: "One of the essential functions of the utopic image is to make apparent a wish in a *free* image of itself, in an image that can play in opposition to the fantasy, which is an inert, blocked, and recurrent image."

Disneyland and international law appear utopian to their visitors by re-presenting extant reality in mythical form,[540] "immobiliz[ing it] in ideology … [and] paper[ing] over the contradictions."[541] Visitors are pulled into this ideology and reality's "contradictions" disappear from their view as they play a part in the presentation of the ideology they have paid to consume. "Disneyland is," according to Marin, "the representation of the makeup of contemporary American ideology" and that representation is "put into play" in the theme park as "'stage'."[542] "[T]his 'stage' … is really not a stage" however, because "[t]he visitors to Disneyland" and to international law – those who invest international law with a supposed capacity to secure Utopia, who look to international law to address conflict, human rights abuse, or climate change, in a spirit much like that of the visitors who come to Disneyland in an effort to escape from external, non-Disney reality – "are on stage themselves … actors in the performance in which they act … captured, like a rat in a maze, and … alienated by their part without being aware of performing a part."[543]

The visitor becomes an actor in Disney's show, passing through a series of limits that the theme park imposes on the world's external reality. The first limit is the "parking lot" that symbolises "the visitor's adjustment to a certain system of signs and behaviour, the system of playful symbols, the free field of consumption for nothing, the *passeist* and aleatory tour *in* the show."[544] Next comes the "ticket booths" where the visitor buys "Disneyland money, with which they can take part in 'utopian' life."[545] Visitors are divorced from the real world, "leaving behind the car … [and] abandon[ing] their money,"[546] in a process that "[n]eutraliz[es] both the car and money,"[547] just as the student of international law leaves the 'real' world behind as she learns the language of consistent and uniform state practice and *uti possidetis juris*.

The centre of Disneyland, Main Street USA, is "the locus of [Disneyland's] … societal truth – consumption,"[548] somewhere to "buy, in a nineteenth-century American decor, actual and real commodities with … real, actual money."[549]

---

540 Ibid. 245: "[T]he visitor who has left reality outside finds it again, but as a real 'imaginary': a fixed, stereotyped, powerful fantasy."

541 See Hill quotation at n. 538.

542 Marin, *Utopics* (n. 4) 240.

543 Ibid.

544 Ibid. 242 (emphasis in original).

545 Ibid. 242–243.

546 Ibid. 243.

547 Ibid. 244.

548 Ibid. 247.

549 Ibid. 247.

Main Street USA leads visitors into Fantasyland where visitors encounter "images, characters, and animals of the tales illustrated by Disney in his animated films,"[550] many "made living by their transformation into real materials ... and through their animation by men and women disguised as movie or storybook characters."[551] In Fantasyland "[i]mage ... becomes real, but ... reality is [also] changed into image" so that "the visitor who .. left reality outside finds it again ... as a real 'imaginary': a fixed, stereotyped, powerful fantasy."[552] Here the visitor's Utopian "wish is caught in [fantasy's] ... snare" as "[t]he other side of reality is presented ... in the form of banal, routine images of Disney's films ... the bankrupt signs of an imagination homegenized by the mass media."[553] Marin defines "the fantasy" at work here as "an inert, blocked, and recurrent image" associated with "the collective, totalitarian form taken by the 'imaginary' of a society, blocked by its specular [mirror-like] self-image."[554]

"Disneyland is on the side of the fantasy and not on that of a free or utopic representation."[555] There is nothing negative – nothing that negates – in Disneyland. Visitors are offered a fantastical representation of reality, an image of America's industrial-technological society, a quasi-religious celebration of reality's human-ness. Frontierland, with its "mule-train mines of precious metals and steamboats on the Mississippi,"[556] celebrates "penetration into and victory over the lands of the first inhabitants,"[557] a monument to "the ever-increasing American appropriation of land and resource."[558] Adventureland represents "the outside geographical world" with "primitive cannibals rising on the riverbanks [who] seem to repeat the gestures that Indians made in Frontierland."[559] America's history, as represented in Frontierland, and the geography of places beyond America, as represented in Adventureland, are "assimilated" and "neutralized" by their fantastical representation to Disneyland's visitors;[560] history and geography are brought within and made

550 Ibid. 245.
551 Ibid.
552 Ibid.
553 Ibid. 246.
554 Ibid. 246.
555 Ibid.
556 Ibid. 250.
557 Ibid.
558 Ibid.
559 Ibid.
560 Ibid. 250: "These two districts represent the distances of history and geography, the distance represented inside America in the first [Frontierland], and the distance represented outside in the second [Adventureland]. They are both assimilated because they are shown on the same stage, so to speak; they are thereby neutralized."

subject to human cognition and control as aspects of "a *human world*, entirely made by the human mind."[561]

In the final stage of Disneyfication, Tomorrowland offers the visitor an image of the future centred on "the Carousel of Progress, a gift of the General Electric Corporation":[562]

> [T]he visitor becomes a spectator, immobilized and passive, seated in front of a circular and moving stage that shows successive scenes taken from family life in the nineteenth century, in the beginning of the twentieth century, today, and tomorrow. It is the *same* family that is presented in these different historical periods; the story of this "permanent" family is told to visitors, who no longer narrate their own story. History is neutralized; the scenes only change in relation to the increasing quantity of electric implements, the increasing sophistication of the utensil-dominated human environment.... Men and women adapt perfectly to this environment and "act" mechanically.[563]

Disneyland enacts "[t]he Myth of Technological Progress."[564] The frontier is overcome, the outside is brought inside, and the future is mapped through technologies that guarantee the human-ness of all reality, securing "a [past, present and future] *human world* [that is] entirely made by the human mind."[565]

Like Disneyland, international law offers "the fictional solution to conflicting tensions":[566]

> [I]nternational law's value and its misery lie in its being the fragile surface of political community among social agents – States, other communities, individuals – who disagree about their preferences but do this *within a structure* that invites them to argue in terms of an assumed universality.[567]

The assumption of this "universality" means that an international legal "Utopia is perfectly present, but ... only as a representation ... [whose] harmony exists

561 See Allott quotation at n. 163.
562 Marin, *Utopics* (n. 4) 251.
563 Ibid. 255.
564 Ibid. 254.
565 See Allott quotation at n. 163.
566 See Marin quotation at n. 537.
567 Koskenniemi, "What is International Law For?" (n. 94) 48 (also quoted at n. 94) (emphasis added).

only on [international law's] … [Disney-like] stage,"[568] on its "fragile surface." "[T]he work of utopic fiction" – the utopian aspirations for "World other" illustrated in the work of authors like Le Guin and Robinson – "is embedded and immobilized in an ideological figure" – in the formal structure of international law – "restrict[ing utopia's] … play so that it no longer represents the true conflicts men and women imagine themselves having."[569]

In international law's formal structure, as in Disneyland's theme park, the possibility of a utopian neutralisation of what is in pursuit of "World other" is neutralised by fantastical, degenerate representations of contemporary reality as Utopia. The UN Charter offers the fantasy of a unified global community – "We the peoples of the United Nations"[570] – neutralising the possibility of a truly utopian response to inter-national conflict, grounded in the history of the "true conflicts" between peoples. Despite the probability of global temperature rises in excess of 1.5°C in the relatively short term (2030 to 2052) and the catastrophic consequences that will result,[571] the UNFCCC system – the United Nations Framework Convention on Climate Change (1992),[572] the Kyoto Protocol (1997),[573] and the Paris Agreement (2015)[574] – continues to pursue the objective of "prevent[ing] dangerous anthropogenic interference with the climate system."[575] In doing so the UNFCCC system, like Disneyland, operates "on the side of the fantasy and not on that of a free or utopic representation" of extant reality and the imperative for "World other."[576]

The same can be said of the Convention on Biological Diversity ('CBD').[577] The CBD's preamble affirms 196 states parties' "[d]etermin[ation] to conserve and sustainably use biological diversity for the benefit of present and future

568 Marin, *Utopics* (n. 4) 248.

569 Ibid.

570 Charter of the United Nations (n. 372), preamble.

571 See part 2, section 4.2 ("The Changing Climate") above.

572 United Nations Framework Convention on Climate Change ('UNFCCC'), New York, 9th May 1992, 1771 UNTS 107, available at <https://unfccc.int/resource/docs/convkp/conveng.pdf> (last visited 2nd August 2019).

573 Kyoto Protocol to the United Nations Framework Convention on Climate Change, Kyoto, 11th December 1997, 2303 UNTS 162, available at <https://unfccc.int/resource/docs/convkp/kpeng.pdf> (last visited 2nd August 2019).

574 Paris Agreement, (n. 298).

575 UNFCCC (n. 572), Article 2.

576 "On the side of the fantasy …" – see Marin quotation at n. 555. I have addressed the viability of the UNFCCC system in previous work, developing a similar analysis to that offered here in Nicholson, "Walter Benjamin" (n. 383) 113–114.

577 Convention on Biological Diversity ('CBD'), Rio de Janeiro, 5th June 1992, 1760 UNTS 79.

generations."[578] In 2010 parties to the CBD adopted a set of targets – the "Aichi Biodiversity Targets"[579] – designed to address ongoing global biodiversity loss. The approach taken is illustrated in these two targets:

> Target 5: By 2020, the rate of loss of all natural habitats, including forests, is at least halved and where possible brought close to zero, and degradation and fragmentation is significantly reduced.[580]

> Target 11: By 2020, at least 17 per cent of terrestrial and inland water, and 10 per cent of coastal and marine areas, especially areas of particular importance for biodiversity and ecosystem services, are conserved through effectively and equitably managed, ecologically representative and well connected systems of protected areas and other effective area-based conservation measures, and integrated into the wider landscapes and seascapes.[581]

A 2014 assessment of progress towards the Aichi targets in the journal *Science* was pessimistic: "[D]espite accelerating policy and management responses to the biodiversity crisis, the impacts of these efforts are unlikely to be reflected in improved trends in the state of biodiversity by 2020."[582] The authors' "projections indicate[d] no significant improvement or a worsening situation by 2020, relative to 2010,"[583] and they concluded that "efforts need to be redoubled to positively affect trajectories of change and enable global biodiversity goals to be met by the end of the current decade."[584] This 2014 conclusion is all the more negative when seen in the context of the CBD parties' failure to achieve

578 Ibid., preamble. On the number of state parties see Secretariat of the Convention on Biological Diversity, <https://www.cbd.int/information/parties.shtml> (last visited 2nd August 2019, and number of states parties quoted (196) accurate at that date).

579 Aichi Biodiversity Targets, <https://www.cbd.int/sp/targets/> (last visited 2nd August 2019). The targets were adopted in Convention on Biological Diversity "COP [Conference of the Parties] 10 Decision X/2," <https://www.cbd.int/decision/cop/?id=12268> (last visited 2nd August 2019).

580 Aichi Biodiversity Targets, ibid.

581 Ibid.

582 Derek P. Tittensor, Matt Walpole, Samantha L.L. Hill, Daniel G. Boyce *et al.*, "A mid-term analysis of progress toward international biodiversity targets" (2014) 346 (6206) *Science* 241, 241.

583 Ibid. 242.

584 Ibid. 244.

their previous 2002 target of a significant reduction in the rate of biodiversity loss by 2010.[585]

Notwithstanding past and (in 2014) projected future failure to meet global biodiversity targets, a May 2018 paper in *Science* calls for another set of global biodiversity targets, using the Paris Climate Change Agreement as a template for a new "global deal."[586] The IPCC's report on the impacts of global warming above 1.5°C, discussed above,[587] was released in October 2018, approximately five months after this *Science* paper's publication. The October report makes the improbability of achieving the Paris climate targets, and the inadequacy of those targets even if they are achieved, clear.[588] And yet, at around the same time, the May 2018 *Science* paper is optimistic about the "flexible architecture" of the Paris Agreement and the possibility of combining that architecture with an enhanced contribution from the private sector:[589]

> [I]f they join the [new global biodiversity] accord [that the 2018 paper calls for], leading corporations and associations in the sea-food, forestry, agricultural, and insurance industries should be involved in establishing the targets for marine, terrestrial, and coastal habitat and biodiversity conservation.... [A]s part of the global agreement for biodiversity, individual companies should pledge their own business targets, policies, and timelines for attaining the overall industry goal.[590]

Thought and action have become so insulated from the fundamental, systemic nature of present reality, so dominated by postmodern consumption and commodification,[591] that even in the face of an inescapably systemic

---

585 Secretariat of the Convention on Biological Diversity, *Global Biodiversity Outlook 3* (Montreal, 2010), <https://www.cbd.int/doc/publications/gbo/gbo3-final-en.pdf> (last visited 2nd August 2019), at 5 ("Foreword by the United Nations Secretary-General"): "In 2002, the world's leaders agreed to achieve a significant reduction in the rate of biodiversity loss by 2010. Having reviewed all available evidence, including national reports submitted by Parties, this third edition of the *Global Biodiversity Outlook* concludes that the target has not been met."

586 Edward B. Barbier, Joanne C. Burgess, and Thomas J. Dean, "How to pay for saving biodiversity: Can private sector involvement in a global agreement help to conserve global biodiversity?" (2018) 360 (6388) *Science* 486.

587 See text at n. 298 to n. 303.

588 See ibid.

589 Barbier *et al.*, (n. 586) 487.

590 Ibid. 488.

591 On the "fundamental, systemic nature of present reality" and "postmodern consumption and commodification" see text at n. 33 to n. 43.

environmental crisis and a failure to achieve past global biodiversity targets an extension of the extant system's consumptive, commodified, corporate logic is seen, in this May 2018 paper, as the appropriate response. The reality of a future which does not involve ever increasing rates of biodiversity loss is represented, formalised and institutionalised in the CBD's texts, processes, and secretariat so that it "becomes real, but ... [in the process] reality is [also] changed into image";[592] so that global social and political engagement with biodiversity loss becomes a formal, legal, technical exercise of targets, targets, and more targets. In this way the CBD operates "on the side of the [stultifying, self-perpetuating] fantasy" that global biodiversity loss can be addressed in ways that do not involve direct confrontation with *the* system of commodification and consumption.[593] In this way, like the UN Charter and the UNFCCC system, the CBD is "an inert, blocked and recurrent image,"[594] a "degenerate utopia."

The UN's Sustainable Development Goals ('SDGs') are perhaps the most compelling example of international legal governance and norm-setting as a Disney-esque "degenerate utopia." Reviving the UN Charter's "[w]e the peoples" for the twenty-first century – despite being authored by "the Heads of State and Government and High Representatives, meeting at the United Nations Headquarters in New York from 25 to 27 September 2015"[595] – the SDGs insist that "it is 'we the peoples' who are embarking ... on the road to 2030" through "an Agenda of the people, by the people and for the people."[596] Promising a utopia of "'win-win' cooperation which can bring huge gains to all countries and all parts of the world,"[597] this is a "Tomorrowland" of unprecedented global co-operation and progress across the full range of governance issues (poverty, food security, gender equality, access to water, energy security, and climate change, to name just some).[598]

The SDGs commit the "peoples" of the world to, for example, "[e]nd[ing] poverty in all its forms everywhere" / "[b]y 2030, eradicat[ing] extreme poverty for all people everywhere, currently measured as people living on less

592 "Becomes real ..." – see Marin quotation at n. 552.

593 "On the side ..." – see Marin quotation at n. 555.

594 Marin, *Utopics* (n. 4) 246.

595 United Nations General Assembly Resolution 70/1, "Transforming our world: the 2030 Agenda for Sustainable Development," UN Doc A/Res/70/1, available at <http://research.un.org/en/docs/ga/quick/regular/70> (last visited 2nd August 2019), paragraph 1.

596 Ibid., paragraph 52.

597 Ibid., paragraph 18.

598 "Tomorrowland" – see text at n. 562 to n. 563.

than $1.25 a day."[599] The two versions of the goal – one without the qualifier "extreme" and the quantifier "$1.25 a day," the other with – reflect the need for a poster version, on sale in something like the Main Street USA gift shop,[600] and a policy-speak version for implementation and verification. After all, outright opposition to "poverty" *per se* sells better than mere qualified opposition to "extreme poverty."

The SDGs respond indirectly to Philip Allott's call for a "re-imagin[ation of] the human world."[601] They are a programme, akin to Allott's draft treaties in *Eunomia*,[602] based on the assumption that reality is human and that a better world can be built through the codification of collective intentions.[603] Allott's faith in a unified global community is more strident than the SDGs' – he prefers "we, the people" to the UN Charter's and SDGs' "we the peoples" because,[604] in his view, "[i]nternational society is the society of the whole human race and the society of all societies."[605] But the phrasing in his 1990 draft treaties ("[w]e undertake to do everything possible to eliminate the practice of war") anticipates the tone and style of the SDGs ("[w]e are determined to end poverty and hunger, in all their forms and dimensions").[606]

Like Disneyland, the SDGs re-present extant reality as a fantasy of ongoing human progress: "Within the past generation, hundreds of millions of people have emerged from extreme poverty ... The spread of information and communications technology and global interconnectedness has great potential to accelerate human progress."[607] In the SDGs there is no sense that the causes of poverty, environmental degradation, or food shortages are systemic; that the conditions in which human beings live are, ultimately, the product of processes of industrialisation, production and commodification that might be bound together under the label 'capitalism.' The SDG's fantasy is sustained and promoted by Project Everyone, "a team of communications and campaigns specialists" founded by film director Richard Curtis (*Four Weddings and A Funeral*, *Love Actually*), "who sit at the heart of a global network of campaigning

599 United Nations General Assembly Resolution 70/1 (n. 595), "Goal 1" at 12.
600 "Main Street USA" – see text at n. 548 to n. 549.
601 See Allott quotation at n. 125.
602 See text at n. 140, n. 141 and n. 142.
603 See Allott quotation at n. 163.
604 "We, the people" – see Allott quotation at n. 139.
605 Allott, *Eunomia* (n. 11) 411 (paragraph 19.27, original in italics).
606 "We undertake to do everything possible ..." – see Allott quotation at n. 141; "We are determined to end poverty ..." – United Nations General Assembly Resolution 70/1 (n. 595) ('Preamble,' under 'People').
607 United Nations General Assembly Resolution 70/1 (n. 595), paragraph 15.

organisations, private sector partners, brands, governments, UN agencies, public figures, and social influencers."[608]

The Global Goals website, constructed by Project Everyone, features one brightly coloured square for each SDG in a format similar, in style and presentation, to Fyre festival's orange tile.[609] Each square contains a few words for each SDG – "No Poverty," "Zero Hunger," "Good Health and Well-Being," "Quality Education," "Gender Equality."[610] The website lists "Bill and Melinda Gates Foundation Goalkeepers" – Ed Sheeran (musician), Emmanuel Macron (President of France), Erna Solberg (Prime Minister of Norway), Melinda Gates ("global advocate for women and girls").[611] Results are measured in the fantastical reality of metrics and "top-tier media" engagement, rather than through peoples' lived experiences:

> Impact and Results: This year [2018] more than 80 journalists from around the world participated in the events and awards, with 300 original stories and opinion pieces written. The event and report were covered by top-tier media titles such as CNN, Vox, Quartz, The Financial Times, The New York Times, National Geographic, Elle, NPR and many more. In addition, over 859k digital engagements with the report content were tracked, 25 million engagements with content from the event, and 530 meaningful actions taken by the Goalkeepers to progress the Goals [the term "meaningful actions" is not defined].[612]

As "on [Disney's] Main Street USA ... reality reemerges in a mediated system of collective representations and figures."[613] In Disneyland, "as the cartoons become real, they also deform and disguise reality,"[614] and the same can be said of the SDGs, with their reduction of reality to metrics, "digital engagements" and "meaningful actions."

In March 2019 it was reported that students on the 'Internet and New Media' course at China's Henan University were required to make at least one thousand new friends on Chinese social media app WeChat in order to pass an

608 See Project Everyone, <http://www.project-everyone.org/> (last visited 2nd August 2019).

609 See text at n. 502.

610 See Global Goals, <https://www.globalgoals.org/> (last visited 2nd August 2019).

611 See Gates Foundation, <https://www.gatesfoundation.org/goalkeepers/> (last visited 2nd August 2019).

612 Project Everyone, <http://www.project-everyone.org/case-studies/goalkeepers-2018/> (last visited 2nd August 2019).

613 Marin, *Utopics* (n. 4) 248.

614 Ibid.

assignment.[615] The thinking behind that assignment echoes Project Everyone's media(ted), metricised logic. Distinguishing lived experience from metrics, a student on the course reportedly commented "WeChat friends are not equal to real friends. Is this not just malicious marketing?"[616] Even if it is there is a very real market for this unreality, as the South China Morning Post reports:

> Some people ... have bought the accounts of WeChat users to mine for data and to use as part of click farms to inflate traffic ... [with] a one month-old WeChat account [selling] for around 55 yuan (US$8.19) but a two year-old WeChat account with real-name registration ... [potentially] cost[ing] around 230 yuan.[617]

Borrowing language from Susan Marks' analysis of the human rights movement – and, to be clear, Marks is not discussing the SDGs here – the SDGs, like the CBD and the UNFCCC system, "keep the focus fixed on individual decisions, policies and behaviours ... [becoming] bound up with the processes of systemic self-reproduction."[618] As Marks notes "change unfolds within a context that includes systematic constraints and pressures,"[619] and yet the SDGs maintain that with sufficient will and cooperation "the journey [will be] ... successful and its gains irreversible."[620] Such "voluntarist modes of thought ... mask the systematicity, and in that sense necessity, of existing configurations of forces and relations"[621] – the systemic causes of poverty, exclusion, domination, environmental degradation, and inequality – creating a "degenerate utopia," a fantastical, theme park re-presentation of reality that neutralises utopian efforts to negate the extant system.

---

615 Sarah Jenkins and Kerry Allen, "Chinese students graded on number of WeChat friends," 13th March 2019, *BBC Trending*, <https://www.bbc.co.uk/news/blogs-trending-47554676> (last visited 2nd August 2019); Lee Jeong-ho, "Chinese university puts students to WeChat test to pass social media course," 17th March 2019, *South China Morning Post*, <https://www.scmp.com/news/china/society/article/3002055/chinese-university-puts-students-wechat-test-pass-social-media> (last visited 2nd August 2019).

616 Jenkins and Allen, n. 615.

617 Lee Jeong-ho, n. 615.

618 Susan Marks, "Human Rights and Root Causes" (2011) 74(1) *Modern Law Review* 57, 72.

619 Ibid. 74.

620 United Nations General Assembly Resolution 70/1 (n. 595) paragraph 53: "The future of humanity and of our planet lies in our hands ... We have mapped the road to sustainable development; it will be for all of us to ensure that the journey is successful and its gains irreversible."

621 Marks, "Human Rights" (n. 618) 74.

Part 4: Towards "World Other"

1 *Exiting International Law's Series*

Thomas Skouteris highlights the structural importance of progressive rhetoric in international law, in an effort to "begin a debate about how [international law's] … professional community constructs / is constructed by progress narratives."[622] Skouteris considers notions of progress in the interwar work of Greek international lawyer Stelios Seferiades, international law's doctrine of sources, and recent growth in the number of international courts and tribunals. He concludes that by "[r]evealing the exclusions of progress narratives and contesting their exclusive right to speak the world 'as it is'" discourse analysis, of the kind undertaken in his book, is a valuable form of "action."[623] His analysis operates "within" international law's structure,[624] reflecting Koskenniemi's call for "critique and contestation" by opening that structure up to debate and challenge.[625]

The "degenerate utopia" perspective presented here is sceptical about the value of such critical inquiries. In opposition to the analysis of existing international legal structures, the analysis offered here posits the admittedly disturbing notion that any understanding of international law limited to its existing, discursive structure will, to a greater or lesser extent, support its continued operation as a distracting fantasy, diverting attention away from the very real imperative for "World other" concretised in the contemporary reality of climate change. Any form of blueprint utopianism – Cassese's, Koskenniemi's, Allott's or Moyn's – misunderstands the utopian inheritance of literature stretching from Thomas More to Ursula Le Guin and Kim Stanley Robinson,[626] presenting Utopia as something to be planned and created when its true, creative function is to hold open the possibility of an exit from or neutralisation of extant social, political, economic and cultural conditions.[627]

In previous work, and in opposition to Susan Marks' emphasis on the need to understand why international law is as it is, I have argued for attempts to write another international law into being, calling for a re-imageination of

622 Thomas Skouteris, *The Notion of Progress in International Law Discourse* (TMC Asser Press, 2010) v.

623 Ibid. 229, and see 227–230 and 218 ("Discourse analysis as action").

624 "Within" – see Koskenniemi quotation at n. 94, and part 2(1) of this article in general.

625 "Critique and contestation" – see Koskenniemi quotation at n. 78.

626 See text at n. 388 to 391.

627 See text at n. 20, n. 379, and part 3, section 3 ("Finding the Exit …").

international law.[628] A re-imageined international law would step beyond existing forms, established traditions and consolidated cultures and, whilst I did not use the language of iconoclasm or utopianism in making that argument, its rejection of existing international law is both iconoclastic and utopian. My argument in this article is, in a sense, a continuation and development of my earlier re-imageination argument, and it re-plays and develops the disagreement, explored as part of my re-imageination argument, with Marks's emphasis on "explanatory analysis."[629]

As a critical perspective Marks' concept of "false contingency" is an invaluable tool for the critique of voluntarist, blueprint perspectives that pay insufficient attention to the social, political, cultural and economic factors that limit prospects for fundamental change.[630] If, however, any capacity international law may have to foster fundamental change is neutralised by the discursive formation of international legal fantasies or "degenerate utopias" that re-present reality as "an inert, blocked, and recurrent image" (the UNFCCC system or the SDGs for example),[631] then analysis of existing structures is insufficient. What is needed, instead, is a theory of the form of practice required to move from what is towards "World other." On that basis I argue that the utopic practice theorised and illustrated in Marin's, Jameson's, Robinson's and Le Guin's work – a practice that actively seeks to get outside the existing structure in an effort to explore the "possibilit[ies] above [the existing] order"[632] – is preferable to critical perspectives, including Marks' argument for "explanatory analysis," that operate within existing international legal discourse.[633]

628 See Nicholson, "Walter Benjamin" (n. 383) 109: "In contrast with Marks' materialist concern to understand 'why' international law is as it is, I take the relatively idealist position that it is possible to think and write an international law that transcends its current anxiety of influence [that is, its anxiety to be faithful to disciplinary influences – methods, practices, texts – from the past] into being."

629 Marks, "Human Rights" (n. 618) 77.

630 On "false contingency" see text at n. 217 and n. 618 to n. 621. See also my treatment of Marks's work and "false contingency" in Nicholson, "Walter Benjamin" (n. 383) 108–109.

631 See Marin quotations at n. 554 and n. 594.

632 See Adorno quotation at n. 62.

633 See Nicholson, "Walter Benjamin" (n. 383) 108: "It is only be risking the discipline [of international law], by abandoning [quoting Benjamin] "the intention of preserving the law itself," that we can truly address international law's violence." See also ibid. 109: "Re-imageination insists that we can make international law into something different from its current material reality by writing that something different into being. Whilst writing it into being will not bring it into being as a material reality – and, in that sense, I agree with Marks that "the meaning of emancipation is not a matter of scholarly fiat but a process of social struggle" [quoting Susan Marks, *The Riddle of All Constitutions:*

In recent work, co-authored with Andrew Lang, Marks advocates fundamental change in international legal discourse, noting the need for a "remaking of the frameworks of knowledge which structure [international lawyers'] ... engagement with the world."[634] Writing in 2017 Lang and Marks suggest that Walter Benjamin's work might hold the key to a re-invention of international legal history "not simply as a set of facts to be known, but as a force to be felt, a secret sympathy to be sensed, and an occasion to be grasped for producing new artefacts that might be used to activate new connections";[635] a re-invention driven by the conviction that "[w]e *can* seize the past and bring it into active relation to the present."[636] Writing in 2015, I argued for a Benjaminian, "allegorical-representational" practice of international law in which:

> there is no set of texts or concepts which the [international legal] practitioner must use; the responsibility for constellating texts, concepts, aspects or fragments of reality to be included in or excluded from [each international legal] representation rests with the practitioner. Everything ever written or created by anyone, anywhere and everything that exists or has ever existed is a potential fragment, to be included in or excluded from the representation. The allegorical-representational practitioner must "immerse himself in the real in order to dislodge its objective interpretation" ... for "truth content is only to be grasped through immersion in the most minute details of subject-matter."[637]

Lang and Marks see critical, transformative potential in Koskenniemi's attachment to international legal form and tradition, embracing the notion that international law "is made up of beliefs, practices, habits and unwritten rules which are handed down and carried forward within the community of international lawyers."[638] They suggest that "Lauterpacht" – that is, early-to-mid twentieth century international lawyer Hersch Lauterpacht, whose work

---

International Law, Democracy, and the Critique of Ideology (OUP, 2000), 137] – writing is the necessary first step to living it."

634 Andrew Lang and Susan Marks, "People With Projects: Writing the Lives of International Lawyers" (2013) 27(2) *Temple International and Comparative Law Quarterly* 437, 452.

635 Andrew Lang and Susan Marks, "Even the Dead Will Not Be Safe: International Law and the Struggle Over Tradition" in Wouter Werner, Marieke De Hoon, and Alexis Galán (eds.), *The Law of International Lawyers: Reading Martti Koskenniemi* (Cambridge University Press, 2017) 321, 335.

636 Ibid. (emphasis in original).

637 Nicholson, "Walter Benjamin" (n. 383) 119–120 (quoting Beatrice Hanssen and Walter Benjamin).

638 Lang and Marks, "Even the Dead" (n. 635) 322.

Koskenniemi considers in the process of building a sense of international law's form and culture[639] – "becomes a 'bridge' which connects us to the past … not just in a symbolic way, but also through our senses."[640]

Whilst Lang and Marks explore the possibility of "producing new artefacts" out of and from within international legal history,[641] I argue that a genuine re-imageination of international law can only be achieved after an exit from the established formal, cultural boundaries of international law. Consistent with that argument, I propose a re-orientation in thinking about international law's ontology, away from an emphasis on form and tradition and towards the notion that international law is a Benjaminian "'idea' … (re)formed in and by every representation,"[642] in and by every international legal argument, every "presentation of an image of what is, what was, and what should be to an audience."[643] This approach, in line with Marin's emphasis on "exiting the series,"[644] is iconoclastically utopian: it is more interested in "the possibility above [the extant] order" than in exploring the history of the extant order.[645]

Consistent with Lang's and Mark's emphasis on "remaking" the structure of international legal practice,[646] Marks explains her analysis of the human rights system as a structure of "planned misery" – "misery that belongs with the logic of particular socio-economic arrangements"[647] – in terms of:

> an emphasis on materialist explanations … that account for phenomena not only in terms of the ideas informing them, but also in terms of their connections to processes of social production … [involving an effort] to delve deeper and ask about the socio-economic conditions within which … ideas were able to develop and gain influence.[648]

For Marks, this approach has a "repoliticising thrust … geared less to problem-solving and the elaboration of remedial proposals … than to the strategic task of channelling grievances into organised and coherent action."[649] Acknowledging that this kind of "explanatory analysis cannot itself specify the forms of

639 See Koskenniemi, *Gentle Civilizer* (n. 529) 353–412.
640 Lang and Marks, "Even the Dead" (n. 635) 327.
641 Ibid. 335.
642 Nicholson, "Walter Benjamin" (n. 383) 124.
643 Ibid. 123.
644 See Marin quotation at n. 20.
645 See Adorno quotation at n. 62.
646 See quotation at n. 634.
647 Marks, "Human Rights" (n. 618) 75.
648 Ibid. 76.
649 Ibid. 76–77.

[organised and coherent] ... action,"[650] Marks argues that it "can be understood in ways that contribute more and less to effective political mobilisation."[651]

To be in any sense "effective" the "explanatory analysis" that Marks promotes would need to generate "political mobilisation" capable of undermining the "mediated system" behind campaigns like Project Everyone's Global Goals initiative.[652] Explanatory analysis and attempts to "[produce] new artefacts" by "activat[ing] new connections" in international legal history cannot,[653] I suggest, contend with the commodified, consumerist power – the sheer marketability – of blueprints and "degenerate utopias." Academic critique of, for example, the "false contingency" behind campaigns like Project Everyone is as intellectually sound as it is socially and politically ineffective.[654] 'No poverty' is a more saleable slogan, than, say, 'let's investigate the social, economic, political, cultural and historic causes of global poverty' – the short version may lack explanatory power but the long version would not fit on a Fyre-style orange tile.[655]

International lawyers 'buy' and invest in utopian blueprints, as the analysis in part two shows, and SDG-type, target-based global governance projects are a global industry. Critical projects within international legal history and "explanatory analysis" of extant social and political structures seem grounded in the supposed susceptibility of marketised reality to rational inquiry, as though that reality was an aspect of social, political and cultural life. *The* postmodern reality is, however, that the market, with its processes of commodification and consumption, sets the terms of contemporary social, political and cultural life, including the limits of what can be achieved through intellectual, explanatory, historical inquiry.[656] The starting point, in these lamentable circumstances, lies not in intellectual analysis *per se* but in an attempt to identify – as my argument for the re-imageination of international law attempts to do – an approach to international law that connects with the contemporary fashion for and sheer marketability of "exiting the series."[657]

650 Ibid. 77.

651 Ibid.

652 "Mediated system" – see Marin quotation at n. 613, and see text at n. 608 to n. 613 generally.

653 "Artefacts" / "connections" – see Lang and Marks quotation at n. 635.

654 On "false contingency" see text at n. 217 and at n. 618 to n. 621.

655 "Orange tile" – see text at n. 502.

656 On this theme see Theodor W. Adorno and Max Horkheimer, "The Culture Industry: Enlightenment as Mass Deception" in Theodor W. Adorno and Max Horkheimer, *Dialectic of Enlightenment* (Verso, 1997 [1944]) 120.

657 "Exiting the series" – see Marin quotation at n. 20.

The foregoing analysis of international legal blueprintism, international law as a "degenerate utopia," and the limitations of critical and historical inquiry within international law, combined with contemporary, postmodern, marketized conditions and the realities of climate change, lead me to suggest that iconoclastic utopianism is the *only* way to maintain the idea that international law offers a path towards a better future. That path runs *via* an exit from what is towards an unspecified, unknowable "World other." As fantasy and science fiction author China Miéville puts it, "if we take utopia seriously, as a total reshaping, its scale means we can't think it from this side. It's the process of making it that will allow us to do so."[658]

Iconoclastic Utopias, involving a run to an exit that leads who-knows-where, sell – think Brexit, Theranos, Fyre, Bolsanaro's Brazil, Erdoğan's Turkey. In his analysis of U.S. mega-retailer Wal-Mart as a curiously utopian entity Fredric Jameson highlights Utopia's contemporary retail value.[659] My ultimate point, inspired by Jameson's Wal-Mart example, and elaborated in the next and final section, is that for international law to play any role in the creation of "World other" it needs to become an iconoclastic marketing tool, representing and promoting a utopian exit from what is. In doing so an iconoclastic, utopian international law must adopt the commodified, consumerist logic of the extant order *purely* as a means of selling and moving towards the "possibility above [that] order."[660] Deborah Cook captures the negative essence of this agenda in her insistence that "[c]riticism of damaged life can do no more than to raise the spectre of what is other, the nonidentical, by using concepts [and, perhaps, examples] that are themselves contaminated by what exists."[661]

The project is not, then, about the "channelling [of] grievances into organised and coherent action" through "explanatory analysis" that highlights extant structures of "planned misery,"[662] for all that this approach has immense *intellectual* value. The project I am proposing involves a deformalized, representational, utopic practice of international law, a practice that draws on "[e]verything ever written or created by anyone, anywhere and everything

658 China Miéville, "The Limits of Utopia," <https://climateandcapitalism.com/2018/03/02/china-mieville-the-limits-of-utopia/> (last visited 2nd August 2019).

659 See Fredric Jameson, "Utopia as Replication" in Fredric Jameson, *Valences of the Dialectic* (Verso, 2010) 410.

660 Adorno, *Negative Dialectics* (n. 62) 397: "An order that shuts itself up in its own meaning will shut itself away from the possibility above order" (also quoted at n. 62, n. 95 and n. 459).

661 Deborah Cook, "From the Actual to the Possible: Nonidentity Thinking" (2005) 12(1) *Constellations* 21, 30.

662 See text at n. 649 to n. 650, and n. 647.

that exists or has ever existed [as] a potential fragment, to be included in or excluded from [each international legal] representation."[663] This is a concept of international law as an iconoclastic marketing tool that re-presents the extant order to itself as an order that is in the process of negating itself, in the hope that such re-presentation expedites the move towards "World other." As Marin puts it, "Utopia is a fictive construction" – a marketing tool, perhaps – "which produces it [Utopia] through determinate (rhetoric-poetic) discursive operations and plays across the narrative as a relatively free and independent representation ... in which, figuratively, the *other* or negative of contemporary social reality appears."[664]

In a sense, by analysing extant international law – the UNFCCC system, the Convention on Biological Diversity, the SDGs – as a "degenerate utopia," I have been trying (and only trying) to make "the *other* or negative" appear. I have, in the course of this article, been attempting to step out of the extant international legal order by engaging with the utopian scholarship of Marin and Jameson, the utopian fiction of Le Guin and Robinson, and the exit-oriented reality of contemporary social phenomena from Brexit to Erdoğan's Turkey, in order to re-present the extant international legal order as a Disneyesque fantasy.[665] Whether my efforts have achieved anything is, of course, not for me to say, but the objective is an *Umfunktionierung*, a "functional transformation" in international legal scholarship:[666] a shift in the function of international legal theory and scholarship from internal inquiry into international legal discourse's own structure, boundaries, history, culture and form, to an external perspective, focused on the societal, representational, mediative, and fantastical impact that extant international law has on contemporary reality.[667] This *Umfunktionierung* is driven by the conviction that the external perspective has a utopian capacity (entirely absent from the internal perspective) to move towards possibilities above and outside the extant order.[668]

663 Nicholson, "Walter Benjamin" (n. 383) 120.

664 Marin, "Theses" (n. 394) 72 (emphasis in original).

665 Rasulov (n. 98) highlights the fantastical quality of international law (see Rasulov quotation in n. 101) but – contrary to the approach advocated here – invests in the extant international legal structure (see Rasulov quotation in n. 98).

666 "*Umfunktionierung*" / "functional transformation" – see text at n. 190 to n. 191.

667 This is, as discussed above, consistent with my argument in Nicholson, "Walter Benjamin" (n. 383).

668 Adorno, *Negative Dialectics* (n. 62) 397: "An order that shuts itself up in its own meaning will shut itself away from the possibility above order" (also quoted at n. 62, n. 95, n. 459 and n. 660).

> [I]f thinking is to be true – if it is to be true today, in any case – it must also be a thinking against itself.[669]

2 *Selling the Negation*

Jameson conceptualises Wal-Mart as:

> the contemporary version of what Marx called the negation of the negation ... not an aberration or an exception, but rather the purest expression of that dynamic of capitalism which devours itself, which abolishes the market by means of the market itself.[670]

Reciting various allegations against this mega-business – that it "drives local businesses under," "reduces available jobs," "scarcely pay[s] a living wage ... is anti-union (except in China)," "hires illegal immigrants," "increasingly emphasizes part-time work," "drives American businesses abroad," "promotes sweatshops and child labor outside the country," "exercises a reign of terror over its own suppliers," and "destroys whole ecologies abroad and whole communities here in the US"[671] – Jameson situates Wal-Mart within a wider global system. That system involves "the so-called bar code" that stores and transmits vast amounts of information.[672] It also involves "containerization ... a revolution in transport" providing a common means of transport – the shipping container – for all types, sizes and shapes of commodity,[673] replacing the disordered process of longshoremen packing individual items into a ship's hold with identical cranes in virtually identical ports loading identical boxes onto virtually identical ships.[674]

In the words of "a nameless CEO ... 'they [Wal-Mart] have killed free-market capitalism in America'."[675] "[N]ot an aberration or an exception,"[676] Jameson identifies Wal-Mart as "the purest expression of that dynamic of capitalism which devours itself."[677] It has the "capacity to reduce inflation ... and to make life affordable for the poorest Americans" whilst being "the very source of

669 Ibid. 365.
670 Jameson, "Utopia as Replication" (n. 659) 421.
671 Ibid. 420.
672 Ibid. 422.
673 Ibid. 422.
674 See Tim Harford, "The simple steel box that transformed global trade" 9th January 2017, *BBC News*, <https://www.bbc.co.uk/news/business-38305512> (last visited 2nd August 2019).
675 Jameson, "Utopia as Replication" (n. 659) 421, quoting Charles Fishman, *The Wal-Mart Effect* (Penguin, 2006).
676 Ibid. 421.
677 Ibid.

their poverty ... the prime mover in the dissolution of American industrial productivity."[678] In this sense, Wal-Mart is the expression of "the historically unique and dialectical dynamic of capitalism itself as a system."[679] It embodies the "dialectic[al] ... injunction to think the negative and the positive together at one and the same time, in the unity of a single thought,"[680] the need to think against and outside of what is from within it.[681]

Whilst a "moralizing" response to Wal-Mart "wants to have the luxury of condemning this evil without particularly imagining anything else in its place,"[682] the utopian response approaches Wal-Mart:

> as a thought experiment ... [as evidence of] what Raymond Williams calls the emergent, as opposed to the residual – the shape of a Utopian future looming through the mist, which we must seize as an opportunity to exercise the Utopian imagination more fully, rather than an occasion of moralizing judgments or regressive nostalgia.[683]

What Jameson says of Wal-Mart applies, in my view, to Brexit, Theranos, Fyre, Bolsanaro's Brazil, and Erdoğan's Turkey. The desire for an exit, manifested in these situations, calls for something more meaningful than a "moralizing," condemnatory response or a nostalgic evocation of liberal democratic stability (Turkey and Brazil), sovereignty (Brexit), or some notional history of responsible, well-regulated corporations (Theranos and Fyre). These situations and phenomena speak to the nature and limitations of contemporary reality and the strength of utopian desire for an exit from it. Whilst populist, opportunistic, authoritarian politics and misleading corporate schemes that exist only in the media (Instagram in the case of Fyre, *Fortune* magazine for Theranos) are not to be celebrated,[684] they cannot be wished away.

The sketch of international law as a "degenerate utopia" above needs to be approached in the same way. It cannot be dismissed by condemnation,

678 Ibid.

679 Ibid.

680 Ibid.

681 See Adorno quotation at n. 669.

682 Jameson, "Utopia as Replication" (n. 659) 421.

683 Ibid. 423. Susan Marks endorses an "anti-moralistic" posture in "Human Rights" (n. 618), at 76. Lang and Marks, "Even the Dead" (n. 635), at 327, note the role of "nostalgia" in international legal history (specifically in the work of Martti Koskenniemi).

684 Jameson, "Utopia as Replication" (n. 659) 433: "I hasten to assure the reader that I do not mean to celebrate Wal-Mart, let alone to forecast the emergence of anything good and progressive from this astonishing new post-monopoly institution.... I have been using [Wal-Mart] ... to illustrate a method."

overcome by a moralising, idealistic response in the style of Philip Allott, or remedied by "regressive nostalgia" for international law's historic form or structure (Koskenniemi and Cassese). It should, I suggest, serve as a stimulus that leads international legal thinkers and practitioners to "experimentally declare positive things which are clearly negative in our own world, to affirm that dystopia is in reality Utopia if examined more closely, [and] to isolate specific features in our empirical present so as to read them as components of a different system."[685]

The failure of the UNFCCC system to provide any viable response to expected global temperature rises in excess of 1.5°C, the failure of the Convention on Biological Diversity to reduce global loss of biodiversity, and the commodified consumerism of the SDGs can be seen as positively negative features of extant international law that make the utopian imperative for "World other" manifest, serving as the fledging "components" – the pre-cursors – "of a different [international legal] system." There will, of course, be numerous other positively negative features within international law. My aim has not been to offer a comprehensive list but to make the case for a methodology, a utopian international legal research agenda, a way of identifying such positively negative features.

This iconoclastic, negative (in the sense that it seeks to negate the extant international legal order) international legal utopianism inverts the realism of blueprint international legal utopianism. Whilst the Cassese and Koskenniemi variety of blueprint international legal utopianism treats extant international law as a frame that fixes the boundaries of possibility, the iconoclastic utopianism advocated here critiques extant international law as a "degenerate utopia." It seeks to identify Wal-Mart-type openings in contemporary reality, cracks in the supposed stability of reality, that offer a chance to exit from what is by demonstrating that extant international law is, in reality, positively negating itself.

It would not, then, be accurate for 'realists' to dismiss iconoclastic utopianism as unrealistic. The better view is that blueprint and iconoclastic variants of utopianism simply have divergent views of the relationship between utopia and reality; divergent views on what reality is and, most importantly, on utopianism's role in determining what is real. Blueprintism maintains that extant reality defines the nature and structure of international law and the extent of its utopianism. Iconoclasm, by contrast, maintains that utopia is a negative, neutralising means of re-presenting reality to itself, in pursuit of its

685 Ibid. 434.

own self-transcendence; a method by which extant international law can think against and outside of itself from within itself.[686]

My aim is not to convince those committed to a blueprint perspective that the iconoclastic perspective presented here ought to be preferred – I doubt even an article this long can shake their commitment. My aim is to establish and promote an iconoclastic perspective that has, to date, been almost entirely absent from international legal theory. Without this perspective international legal thinkers and practitioners are caught in "the ideological closure of the system in which we are somehow trapped and confined" and,[687] more importantly, international law – as a field of intellectual inquiry, and as a practical, professional endeavour – is incapable of moving extant reality towards "World other" because of its status as a "degenerate utopia."

The divergence between blueprint and iconoclastic forms of utopianism centres on historical method. The utopianism advocated here involves "a reawakening of that historicity which our [extant] system – offering itself as the very end of history – necessarily represses and paralyzes."[688] Blueprintism reflects an anti-utopian posture of the kind developed by Popper, Berlin and Arendt, imprisoning thought and practice in well-recognised realities and forms,[689] for fear that their overthrow would "sacrifice ... present generations for some future utopian state."[690] This fear connects with an anti-modern sentiment "in liberal as well as in conservative culture" that is suspicious of "mass culture," the urban, the industrial, and all forms of collectivism (most obviously, socialism and communism).[691]

That anti-modern sentiment leads to a "standard way of dealing with ... social anxieties" – a blueprintism – that "assur[es] us that in whatever future 'more perfect society' all of the negative features it enumerates will have been corrected" through a nostalgic return to what was based of the condemnation of what is.[692] This can be seen, for example, in Moyn's call for a return to a properly politicised, pre-1970s human rights as a replacement for a post-1970s depoliticized, formal human rights;[693] in Allott's insistence on the value of classical, Enlightenment political philosophy and the capacity of the human

686 On "method" see Jameson quotation in n. 684, and on "thinking against" see Adorno quotation at n. 669.
687 "The ideological closure ..." – see Jameson quotation at n. 7.
688 Jameson, "Utopia as Replication" (n. 659) 434.
689 See text at n. 205 to n. 215.
690 Jameson, "Utopia as Replication" (n. 659) 425.
691 Ibid. 426.
692 Ibid. 427.
693 See part 2(4) of this article.

mind to re-create reality, in place of the fallen reality of contemporary life and law, including his attack on 'mass culture' in the form of "bad art and popular culture";[694] and in Koskenniemi's evocation of a lost, historic international legal formalism that offers the key to a revival in international legal culture.[695]

The process of correction involves "so many obedient replacements of the reigning negative terms by their positive opposites"[696] – Jacobin, socialist politics in place of post-1970s formalist, minimalist human rights (Moyn); Enlightenment philosophy and its ideal of human self-(re)creation in place of the chaos of postmodernity (Allott); a commitment to international law's form in place of international legal pragmatism (Koskenniemi). A "negative diagnosis" is the foundation and essence of this regressively nostalgic blueprint utopianism,[697] but the negativity of the diagnosis has "priority" over the positive blueprint prescription that emerges from it.[698] If negativity is, then, the source or origin of Utopia blueprints of what will replace that which is negated are, at best, a secondary feature of the utopian.

The twentieth century anti-urban, anti-collectivist sentiment underpinning blueprint utopianism is, Jameson argues, incompatible with the urban, collectivist reality of "postmodernity and globalisation" apparent in "world population explosion … desertion of the countryside and the growth of the mega-city, global warming and ecological catastrophe … [and] the universal emergence of small-group politics of all kinds."[699] A utopianism consonant with this postmodern, globalised reality involves a move "from anxiety to affirmation,"[700] a "resituating in a more positive way [of] … contemporary denunciations of contemporary society in terms of the spectacle … and the simulacrum."[701]

Embracing the spectacular and the simulated necessitates a re-appraisal of "mass culture" – a re-appraisal of Wal-Mart, Project Everyone and the Global Goals campaign, the "degenerate utopia" of Disneyland, the exit-oriented utopianism of Brexit, Theranos, Fyre, Bolsanaro's Brazil and Erdoğan's Turkey, and the manifest belief in international law as a blueprint for a better future. "Mass

694 "Bad art and popular culture" – see Allott quotation at n. 182, and see part 2(3) of this article.
695 See part 2(1) of this article and text at n. 529 to n. 537.
696 Jameson, "Utopia as Replication" (n. 659) 427.
697 "Negative diagnosis" – ibid. 427; "regressively nostalgic" – see Jameson quotation at n. 683 (referring to "regressive nostalgia").
698 Jameson, "Utopia as Replication" (n. 659) 427: "[The] very reactivity of the Heideggerian response tends to confirm the priority of the negative diagnosis in the first place."
699 Ibid. 428.
700 Ibid.
701 Ibid. 429.

culture" is to be seen as "'an industry of the means of production,'"[702] something at work, for better or worse, on the process of creating society and reality, "an enactment of collective sharing and participation."[703]

The task for international legal thought and practice is not, then, to replace what is with a utopian blueprint of how it ought to be, nor is it to critique contemporary legal-social reality through "explanatory analysis" designed to spark "effective political mobilisation."[704] The task is to sell mass culture's ongoing self-negation to a mass cultural audience, deliberately misappropriating the methods of Project Everyone in a marketing campaign that sells extant international law's self-negation to the widest possible audience. The message we should be selling is that international law has no blueprint for utopia, no plan for a better future; that the UNFCCC system is not going to avert catastrophic climate change; that a cataclysmic loss of biodiversity will not be averted through the Convention on Biological Diversity; that the Sustainable Development Goals will not end poverty.

I am suggesting that international lawyers should stop telling positive stories about the nature, capacity and achievements of international law because doing so perpetuates a "fixed, stereotyped, powerful [mass culture] fantasy" of international law as the means of securing a better global future.[705] In place of such fantastical degeneracy international lawyers should, I suggest, offer detailed accounts of extant international law's inability to address the most fundamental challenges, from climate change to global poverty, as evidence of the very beginnings of something beyond extant international law, something "World other."

Such negative, neutralising, truly utopian accounts would serve as "contribution[s] to the reawakening of the imagination of possible and alternative futures;"[706] attempts to turn the "consumers" – the scholars and practitioners – of extant international law into the "producers" of an international law connected to and evolving in response to the negativity of contemporary reality.[707] The project I am proposing is underpinned by a sense that it is time to "go somewhere else … [to] have another goal …[to] walk a different road … [to] stop following the road [we]'re on, in either direction … [and to] break the circle."[708]

702 Ibid. (quoting Paolo Virno).

703 Ibid.

704 See Marks quotations at n. 650 and n. 651.

705 "Fixed, stereotyped …" – see Marin quotation at n. 552.

706 Jameson, "Utopia as Replication" (n. 659) 434.

707 See quotation from and discussion of Benjamin at n. 193.

708 Le Guin, *The Left Hand* (n. 419) 132 (also quoted at n. 447).

If "[l]ight is the left hand of darkness, and darkness the right hand of light,"[709] then walking through the cold negativity of contemporary reality's darkness offers the best chance of finding international legal light.

Bibliography

Abensour, Miguel, "Persistent Utopia" (2008) 15 *Constellations* 406.

Adorno, Theodor W., *Negative Dialectics* (Continuum, 2007 [1966]).

Adorno, Theodor W. and Max Horkheimer, "The Concept of Enlightenment" in Theodor W. Adorno and Max Horkheimer, *Dialectic of Enlightenment* (Verso, 1997, [1944]) 3.

Adorno, Theodor W. and Max Horkheimer, "The Culture Industry: Enlightenment as Mass Deception" in Theodor W. Adorno and Max Horkheimer, *Dialectic of Enlightenment* (Verso, 1997 [1944]) 120.

Adorno, Theodor, *Minima Moralia: Reflections from Damaged Life* (Verso, 2005 [1951]).

Adorno, Theodor and Max Horkheimer, *Towards a New Manifesto* (Verso 2011).

Allott, Philip, *Eunomia: New Order for a New World* (Oxford University Press, 2001 [paperback edition, first published in 1990]).

Allott, Philip, "Globalisation from above: Actualising the ideal through law" in Philip Allott, *The Health of Nations: Society and Law beyond the State* (Cambridge University Press, 2002) 70.

Allott, Philip, *Eutopia* (Edward Elgar, 2016).

Alston, Philip, "The United Nations: No Hope for Reform?" in Antonio Cassese (ed.), *Realizing Utopia: The Future of International Law* (Oxford University Press, 2012) 38.

Alston, Philip, "Does the Past Matter? On the Origins of Human Rights" (2013) 126 *Harvard Law Review* 2043.

Anderson, Perry, "Bolsanaro's Brazil" (2019) 41(3) *London Review of Books* 11.

Anghie, Antony, "The Evolution of International Law: colonial and postcolonial realities" (2006) 27(5) *Third World Quarterly* 739.

Anghie, Antony, "Whose Utopia? Human Rights, Development and the Third World" (2013) 22(1) *Qui Parle* 63.

Barbier, Edward B., Joanne C. Burgess, and Thomas J. Dean, "How to pay for saving biodiversity: Can private sector involvement in a global agreement help to conserve global biodiversity?" (2018) 360(6388) *Science* 486.

Bauman, Zygmunt, "Utopia with No Topos" (2003) 16(1) *History of the Human Sciences* 23.

Benhabib, Seyla, "Moving beyond False Binarisms: On Samuel Moyn's The Last Utopia" (2013) 22(1) *Qui Parle* 81.

709 Ibid. 199 (also quoted at n. 455).

Benjamin, Walter (Howard Eiland and Kevin McLaughlin tr.), *The Arcades Project* (Belknap Press of Harvard University Press, 2002).

Benjamin, Walter, "On the Concept of History" in Walter Benjamin (Howard Eiland and Michael W. Jennings eds.), *Selected Writings: Volume 4 1938–1940* (Belknap Press of Harvard University Press, 2006) 389.

Benjamin, Walter, "The Author as Producer" in Michael W. Jennings, Howard Eiland and Gary Smith (eds.), *Walter Benjamin: Selected Writings, Volume 2, part 2, 1931–1934* (Belknap Press of Harvard University Press, 2005) 768.

Betzold, Carola, "Adapting to climate change in small island developing states" (2015) 133(3) *Climatic Change* 481.

Blickley, Leigh, "'Hell Has No Wrath Like a Millennial Scorned': Lawyer Suing Fyre Festival Gives Updates on Case" *Huffington Post*, 17th January 2019, <https://www.huffingtonpost.co.uk/entry/fyre-festival-documentaries-laywer_us_5c3e5d70e4b0922a21d9984d?ec_carp=7365817290276570262&guccounter=1> (last visited 2nd August 2019).

Buck Morss, Susan, *The Dialectics of Seeing: Walter Benjamin and the Arcades Project* (MIT Press, 1991).

Búrca, Gráinne de, "Samuel Moyn, *Not Enough: Human Rights in an Unequal World*" (review) (2018) 16(4) *International Journal of Constitutional Law* 1347.

Carty, Anthony, "Social Theory and the 'Vanishing' of International Law: A Review Article" (1992) 41 *International and Comparative Law Quarterly* 939.

Cassese, Antonio (ed.), *Realizing Utopia: The Future of International Law* (Oxford University Press, 2012).

Cassese, Antonio, "Introduction" in Antonio Cassese (ed.), *Realizing Utopia: The Future of International Law* (Oxford University Press, 2012).

Cook, Deborah, "From the Actual to the Possible: Nonidentity Thinking" (2005) 12(1) *Constellations* 21.

COP (Conference of the Parties to the United Nations Framework Convention on Climate Change) 23 website, "How Fiji is Affected by Climate Change," <https://cop23.com.fj/fiji-and-the-pacific/how-fiji-is-affected-by-climate-change/> (last visited 2nd August 2019).

Coscarelli, Joe and Melna Ryzik, "Fyre Festival, a Luxury Music Weekend, Crumbles in the Bahamas" *New York Times*, 28th April 2017, <https://www.nytimes.com/2017/04/28/arts/music/fyre-festival-ja-rule-bahamas.html> (last visited 2nd August 2019).

Davies, William, "Leave, and Leave Again" (2019) 41(3) *London Review of Books* 9.

Douzinas, Costas, "Human Rights and Postmodern Utopia" (2000) 11 *Law and Critique* 219.

Eagleton, Terry, *Ideology: An Introduction* (Verso, 2007 [1991]).

Eckstein, David, Maria-Lena Hutfils, and Maik Winges, "Global Climate Risk Index 2019: Who Suffers Most From Extreme Weather Events? Weather-related Loss Events in

2017 and 1998 to 2017," accessible via <https://www.germanwatch.org/sites/germanwatch.org/files/Global%20Climate%20Risk%20Index%202019_2.pdf> (last visited 2nd August 2019).

Falk, Richard, "The Adequacy of Contemporary Theories of international Law – Gaps in Legal Thinking" (1964) 50(2) *Virginia Law Review* 231.

Fassbender, Bardo, "The Security Council: Progress is Possible but Unlikely" in Antonio Cassese (ed.), *Realizing Utopia: The Future of International Law* (Oxford University Press, 2012) 52.

Feichtner, Isabel, "Realizing Utopia through the Practice of International Law" (2012) 23 *European Journal of International Law* 1143.

Finnis, John, "On Moyn's Christian Human Rights" (2017) 28(1) *King's Law Journal* 12.

Friedell, Deborah, "A chemistry is performed" (2019) 41(3) *London Review of Books* 33.

Füssel, Hans-Martin, "How inequitable is the global distribution of responsibility, capability, and vulnerability to climate change: A comprehensive indicator-based assessment" (2010) 20(4) *Global Environmental Change* 597.

Fyre Festival, "Announcing Fyre Festival," <https://www.youtube.com/watch?v=mz5kY3RsmKo> (last visited 2nd August 2019).

Gates Foundation, <https://www.gatesfoundation.org/goalkeepers/> (last visited 2nd August 2019).

George, Ella, "Purges and Paranoia" (2018) 40(10) *London Review of Books* 22.

Global Goals, <https://www.globalgoals.org/> (last visited 2nd August 2019).

Golder, Ben, "On the genealogy of human rights: an essay on nostalgia" (2016) 22(2) *Australian Journal of Human Rights* 17.

Gray, John, "What Rawls Hath Wrought" (2011) 111(1) *National Interest* 81.

The Guardian, "Fyre festival: creator of disastrous event sentenced on fraud charges," 11th October 2018, <https://www.theguardian.com/us-news/2018/oct/11/fyre-festival-billy-mcfarland-sentenced-prison-fraud> (last visited 2nd August 2019).

Hajjar, Lisa, "Chaos as Utopia: International Criminal Prosecutions as a Challenge to State Power" (2004) 31 *Studies in Law, Politics and Society* 3.

Harford, Tim, "The simple steel box that transformed global trade," 9th January 2017, *BBC News*, <https://www.bbc.co.uk/news/business-38305512> (last visited 2nd August 2019).

Harris, Hunter, "Fyre Festival Was Terrible Before it Even Began" *Vulture*, 5th May 2017, <https://www.vulture.com/2017/05/fyre-festival-fiasco-the-complete-timeline.html> (last visited 2nd August 2019).

Hemptinne, Jérome de, "The Future of International Criminal Justice: A Blueprint for Action" in Antonio Cassese (ed.), *Realizing Utopia: The Future of International Law* (Oxford University Press, 2012) 585.

Hill, Eugene D., "The Place of the Future: Louis Marin and His 'Utopiques'" (1982) 9(2) *Science Fiction Studies* 167.

Huxley, Aldous, *Brave New World* (Chatto & Windus, 1932).

Jacoby, Russell, *Picture Imperfect: Utopian Thought for an Anti-Utopian Age* (Columbia University Press, 2005).

Jameson, Fredric, "Of Islands and Trenches: Naturalization and the Production of Utopian Discourse" (1977) 7(2) *Diacritics* 2.

Jameson, Fredric, *The Political Unconscious: Narrative as a socially symbolic act* (Routledge, 1983).

Jameson, Fredric, *Postmodernism, or The Cultural Logic of Late Capitalism* (Verso, 1991).

Jameson, Fredric, "The Politics of Utopia" (2004) 25 *New Left Review* 35.

Jameson, Fredric, *Archaeologies of the Future: The Desire Called Utopia and Other Science Fictions* (Verso, 2007).

Jameson, Fredric, "The Utopian Enclave" in Fredric Jameson, *Archaeologies of the Future: The Desire Called Utopia and Other Science Fictions* (Verso, 2007) 10.

Jameson, Fredric, "World Reduction in Le Guin" in Fredric Jameson, *Archaeologies of the Future: The Desire Called Utopia and Other Science Fictions* (Verso, 2007) 267.

Jameson, "Progress Versus Utopia, Or Can We Imagine the Future?" in Fredric Jameson, *Archaeologies of the Future: The Desire Called Utopia and Other Science Fictions* (Verso, 2007) 281.

Jameson, Fredric, "'If I Can Find One Good City I Will Spare the Man': Realism and Utopia in Kim Stanley Robinson's *Mars* Trilogy" in Fredric Jameson, *Archaeologies of the Future: The Desire Called Utopia and Other Science Fictions* (Verso, 2007) 393.

Jameson, Fredric, "Utopia as Replication" in Fredric Jameson, *Valences of the Dialectic* (Verso, 2010) 410.

Jameson, Fredric, *The Antinomies of Realism* (Verso, 2013).

Jameson, Fredric, "Coda: Kluge, or, Realism After Affect" in Fredric Jameson, *The Antinomies of Realism* (Verso, 2013) 187.

Jameson, Fredric, "War and Representation" in Fredric Jameson, *The Antinomies of Realism* (Verso, 2013) 232.

Jameson, Fredric, "The Historical Novel Today, Or, Is It Still Possible?" in Fredric Jameson, *The Antinomies of Realism* (Verso, 2013) 259.

Jenkins, Sarah and Kerry Allen, "Chinese students graded on number of WeChat friends," 13th March 2019, *BBC Trending*, <https://www.bbc.co.uk/news/blogs-trending-47554676> (last visited 2nd August 2019).

Jeong-ho, Lee, "Chinese university puts students to WeChat test to pass social media course," 17th March 2019, *South China Morning Post*, <https://www.scmp.com/news/china/society/article/3002055/chinese-university-puts-students-wechat-test-pass-social-media> (last visited 2nd August 2019).

Jouannet, Emmanuelle, "How to Depart from the Existing Dire Condition of Development" in Antonio Cassese (ed.), *Realizing Utopia: The Future of International Law* (Oxford University Press, 2012) 392.

Kiss, Alexandre, "The common heritage of mankind: utopia or reality?" (1985) 40(3) *International Journal* 423.

Kleinman, Zoe, "Has Fyre Festival burned influencers?" *BBC News*, 22nd January 2019, <https://www.bbc.co.uk/news/46945662> (last visited 2nd August 2019).

Koskenniemi, Martti, "*Eunomia: New Order for a New World*" (review), (1993) 87 *American Journal of International Law* 160.

Koskenniemi, Martti, *The Gentle Civilizer of Nations: The Rise and Fall of International Law 1870–1960* (Cambridge University Press, 2001).

Koskenniemi, Martti, *From Apology to Utopia: The Structure of International Legal Argument – Reissue with New Epilogue* (Cambridge University Press, 2005, first published – without epilogue – in 1989).

Koskenniemi, Martti, "International Law as Therapy: Reading the Health of Nations" (2005) 16 *European Journal of International Law* 329.

Koskenniemi, Martti, "What is International Law For?" in Malcolm D. Evans (ed.), *International Law* (4th edition, Oxford University Press, 2014) 29.

Koskenniemi, Martti, "Utopia as Critique" in Antonio Cassese (ed.), *Realizing Utopia: The Future of International Law* (Oxford University Press, 2012) 3.

Laclau, Ernesto and Chantal Mouffe, *Hegemony and Socialist Strategy: Towards a Radical Democratic Politics* (2nd edition, Verso, 2001).

Lafontaine, Fannie, "Universal Jurisdiction – the Realistic Utopia" (2012) 10 *Journal of International Criminal Justice* 1277.

Lang, Andrew and Susan Marks, "People With Projects: Writing the Lives of International Lawyers" (2013) 27(2) *Temple International and Comparative Law Quarterly* 437.

Lang, Andrew and Susan Marks, "Even the Dead Will Not Be Safe: International Law and the Struggle Over Tradition" in Wouter Werner, Marieke De Hoon, and Alexis Galán (eds.), *The Law of International Lawyers: Reading Martti Koskenniemi* (Cambridge University Press, 2017) 321.

Latour, Bruno, *Down to Earth* (Polity, 2018).

Lemaitre, Julieta, "The View from Somewhere: on Samuel Moyn's Not Enough," 9th July 2018, *Law and Political Economy* <https://lpeblog.org/2018/07/09/the-view-from-somewhere-on-samuel-moyns-not-enough/> (last visited 2nd August 2019).

Levin, Kelly, World Resources Institute, "Half a Degree and a World Apart: The Difference in Climate Impacts Between 1.5°C and 2°C of Warming," 7th October 2018, <https://www.wri.org/blog/2018/10/half-degree-and-world-apart-difference-climate-impacts-between-15-c-and-2-c-warming> (last visited 2nd August 2019).

Le Guin, Ursula, *The Lathe of Heaven* (Gollancz, 2001 [1971]).

Le Guin, Ursula, *The Left Hand of Darkness* (Orbit, 1981 [1969]).

Levitas, Ruth, "For Utopia: The (Limits of the) Utopian Function in Late Capitalist Society" (2000) 3(2–3) *Critical Review of International Social and Political Philosophy* 25.

Livingstone, Josephine, "Fyre Festival Was a Huge Scam. Is Netflix's Fyre Documentary a Scam, Too?" *The New Republic*, 12th February 2019, <https://newrepublic.com/article/153095/fyre-festival-huge-scam-netflixs-fyre-documentary-scam-too> (last visited 2nd August 2019).

Manfredi, Zak, "Compatibility as Complicity? On Neoliberalism and Human Rights" 28th May 2018, *Law and Political Economy* <https://lpeblog.org/2018/05/28/compatibility-as-complicity-on-neoliberalism-and-human-rights/#more-707> (last visited 2nd August 2019).

Mantena, Karuna, "Gettting the NIEO Right," 21st May 2018, *Law and Political Economy*, <https://lpeblog.org/2018/05/21/getting-the-nieo-right/#more-701> (last visited 2nd August 2019).

Marin, Louis (Fredric Jameson trans.), "Theses on Ideology and Utopia" (1976) 6 *Minnesota Review* 71.

Marin, Louis (Robert A. Vollrath tr.), *Utopics: Spatial Play* (Humanities Press, 1984).

Marin, Louis, "Frontiers of Utopia: Past and Present" (1993) 19(3) *Critical Inquiry* 397.

Marks, Susan, "False Contingency" (2009) 62 *Current Legal Problems* 1.

Marks, Susan, "Human Rights and Root Causes" (2011) 74(1) *Modern Law Review* 57.

Massimo, Elisa (President and Chief Executive of Human Rights First), Letter to the Editor of the New York Times, 29th April 2018, <https://www.nytimes.com/2018/04/29/opinion/human-rights.html> (last visited 2nd August 2019).

Melzer, Nils, "Bolstering the Protection of Civilians in Armed Conflict" in Antonio Cassese (ed.), *Realizing Utopia: The Future of International Law* (Oxford University Press, 2012) 508.

Miéville, China, "The Limits of Utopia," <https://climateandcapitalism.com/2018/03/02/china-mieville-the-limits-of-utopia/> (last visited 2nd August 2019).

Milman, Oliver, "World 'nowhere near on track' to avoid warming beyond 1.5C target," 27th September 2018, *The Guardian*, <https://www.theguardian.com/environment/2018/sep/26/global-warming-climate-change-targets-un-report> (last visited 2nd August 2019).

Mishra, Pankaj, "The Mask It Wears" (2018) 40(12) *London Review of Books* 9.

Moyn, Samuel, *The Last Utopia: Human Rights in History* (Belknap Press of Harvard University Press, 2010).

Moyn, Samuel, *Human Rights and the Uses of History* (Verso, 2014).

Moyn, Samuel, "Epilogue: The Future of Human Rights" in Moyn, *Human Rights and the Uses of History* (Verso, 2014) 135.

Moyn, Samuel, *Christian Human Rights* (University of Pennsylvania Press, 2015).

Moyn, Samuel, *Not Enough: Human Rights in an Unequal World* (Belknap Press of Harvard University Press, 2018).

Moyn, Samuel, "How the Human Rights Movement Failed," 23rd April 2018, *New York Times*, <https://www.nytimes.com/2018/04/23/opinion/human-rights-movement-failed.html> (last visited 2nd August 2019).

Moyn, Samuel, "The Alt-Right's Favorite Meme is 100 Years Old," 13th November 2018, *New York Times* <https://www.nytimes.com/2018/11/13/opinion/cultural-marxism-anti-semitism.html> (last visited 2nd August 2019).

Moyn, Sam, "Bias and Exclusion in Human Rights History," 13th August 2018, *Law and Political Economy*, <https://lpeblog.org/2018/08/13/bias-and-exclusion-in-human-rights-history/> (last visited 2nd August 2019).

NASA, "Mars Terraforming Not Possible Using Present-Day Technology," 30th July 2018, <https://www.nasa.gov/press-release/goddard/2018/mars-terraforming> (last visited 2nd August 2019).

The Nation, <https://www.thenation.com/authors/samuel-moyn/> (last visited 2nd August 2019).

Netflix (documentary film), "Fyre: The Greatest Party that Never Happened," <https://www.netflix.com/gb/title/81035279> (last visited 2nd August 2019).

Nicholson, Matthew, "Walter Benjamin and the Re-Imageination of International Law" (2016) 27 *Law and Critique* 103.

Nicholson, Matthew, "Majority Rule and Human Rights: Identity and Non-Identity in SAS v France" (2016) 67(2) *Northern Ireland Legal Quarterly* 115.

Nicholson, Matthew, "Psychoanalyzing International Law(yers)" (2017) 18(3) *German Law Journal* 441.

O'Connell, Paul, "Capitalism, Inequality and Human Rights," 4th June 2018, *Law and Political Economy*, <https://lpeblog.org/2018/06/04/capitalism-inequality-and-human-rights/> (last visited 2nd August 2019).

Ovenden, Olivia, "Fyre Festival Was An Even Bigger Shitshow Than We Thought" *Esquire*, <https://www.esquire.com/uk/culture/a25854517/fyre-festival-was-an-even-bigger-shitshow-than-we-thought/> (last visited 2nd August 2019).

Parloff, Roger, "This CEO is out for blood" *Fortune*, 12th June 2014 <http://fortune.com/2014/06/12/theranos-blood-holmes/> (last visited 2nd August 2019).

Parloff, Roger, "How Theranos Misled Me" *Fortune*, 17th December 2015 <http://fortune.com/2015/12/17/how-theranos-misled-me-elizabeth-holmes/> (last visited 2nd August 2019).

Peters, Anne, "Are we Moving towards Constitutionalization of the World Community?" in Antonio Cassese (ed.), *Realizing Utopia: The Future of International Law* (Oxford University Press, 2012) 118.

Popper, Karl, "Utopia and Violence" (1986) 149(1) *World Affairs* 3.

Project Everyone, <http://www.project-everyone.org/> (last visited 2nd August 2019).

Rasulov, Akbar, "The Utopians" in Jean d'Aspremont and Sahib Singh (eds.), *Concepts for International Law: Contributions to Disciplinary Thought* (Edward Elgar, 2019) 879.

Robinson, Darryl, "Inescapable Dyads: Why the International Criminal Court Cannot Win" (2015) 28 *Leiden Journal of International Law* 323.

Robinson, Kim Stanley, 'Remarks on Utopia in the Age of Climate Change' (2016) 27 *Utopian Studies* 2.

Rocha, Maria, Mario Krapp, Johannes Guetschow, Louise Jeffery, Bill Hare, and Michiel Schaeffer, "Historical Responsibility for Climate Change – from countries emissions to contributions to temperature increase," November 2015, <https://climateanalytics.org/media/historical_responsibility_report_nov_2015.pdf> (last visited 2nd August 2019).

Schwarzenberger, Georg, "Jus Pacis Ac Belli?: Prolegomena to a Sociology of International Law" (1943) 37(3) *American Journal of International Law* 460.

Sealey-Huggins, Leon, "'1.5°C to stay alive': climate change, imperialism and justice for the Caribbean" (2017) 38(11) *Third World Quarterly* 2444.

Secretariat of the Convention on Biological Diversity, <https://www.cbd.int/information/parties.shtml> (last visited 2nd August 2019).

Secretariat of the Convention on Biological Diversity, *Global Biodiversity Outlook 3* (Montreal, 2010), <https://www.cbd.int/doc/publications/gbo/gbo3-final-en.pdf> (last visited 2nd August 2019).

Secretariat of the United Nations Framework Convention on Climate Change, <https://unfccc.int/process/the-paris-agreement/status-of-ratification> (last visited 2nd August 2019).

Skouteris, Thomas, *The Notion of Progress in International Law Discourse* (TMC Asser Press, 2010).

Tittensor, Derek P., Matt Walpole, Samantha L.L. Hill, Daniel G. Boyce *et al.*, "A mid-term analysis of progress toward international biodiversity targets" (2014) 346 (6206) *Science* 241.

Victoria, Francisci de (Ernest Nys ed.), *De Indis et De ivre belli relectiones being parts of Reflectiones Theologicae XII* (The Carnegie Institution of Washington, 1917).

Weller, Marc, "The Real Utopia: International Constitutionalism and The Use of Force" in Robert Schütze (ed.), *Globalization and Governance: International Problems, European Solutions* (Cambridge University Press, 2018) 131.

Wong, Poh Poh, "Small island developing states" (2011) 2(1) *WIREs Climate Change* 1.

United Nations Department of Economic and Social Affairs, "World Population Prospects: The 2017 Revision," 21st June 2017, <https://www.un.org/development/desa/publications/world-population-prospects-the-2017-revision.html> (last visited 2nd August 2019).

Werlin, Juliette, "Nowhere Now: Thomas More's 'Utopia' at 500" *Los Angeles Review of Books*, <https://lareviewofbooks.org/article/nowhere-now-thomas-mores-utopia-at-500/> (last visited 2nd August 2019).

The White House, "Statement by President Trump on the Paris Accord," 1st June 2017, <https://www.whitehouse.gov/briefings-statements/statement-president-trump-paris-climate-accord/> (last visited 2nd August 2019).

Wilde, Ralph, *International Territorial Administration: How Trusteeship and the Civilizing Mission Never Went Away* (Oxford University Press, 2008).

World Resources Institute, "Adaptation Finance Accountability Initiative," <https://www.wri.org/our-work/project/adaptation-finance-accountability-initiative> (last visited 2nd August 2019).

Cases and Legal Materials

Agreement Governing the Activities of States on the Moon and Other Celestial Bodies, 610 UNTS 305 (no. 8843).

Aichi Biodiversity Targets, <https://www.cbd.int/sp/targets/> (last visited 2nd August 2019).

Antarctic Treaty, 402 UNTS 71 (no. 5778).

Belgin Dogru v France (2008) 39 EHRR 179.

Charter of the United Nations, San Francisco, 26th June 1945, available at <https://www.un.org/en/charter-united-nations/> (last visited 2nd August 2019).

Convention on Biological Diversity ('CBD'), Rio de Janeiro, 5th June 1992, 1760 UNTS 79.

Convention on Biological Diversity, "COP [Conference of the Parties] 10 Decision X/2," <https://www.cbd.int/decision/cop/?id=12268> (last visited 2nd August 2019).

Dahlab v Switzerland, Application No 42393/98, unreported, <http://hudoc.echr.coe.int/sites/eng/pages/search.aspx?i=001-22643#{"itemid":["001-22643"]}>.

IPCC, 2018, "Summary for Policymakers" in V. Masson-Delmotte, P. Zhai, H.-O. Pörtner, D. Roberts, J. Skea, P.R. Shukla, A. Pirani, Moufouma-Okia, C. Péan, R. Pidcock, S. Connors, J.B.R. Matthews, Y. Chen, X. Zhou, M.I. Gomis, E. Lonnoy, Maycock, M. Tignor, and T. Waterfield (eds.), "Global Warming of 1.5°C. An IPCC Special Report on the impacts of global warming of 1.5°C above pre-industrial levels and related global greenhouse gas emission pathways, in the context of strengthening the global response to the threat of climate change, sustainable development, and efforts to eradicate poverty" (*World Meteorological Organization*), accessible via <https://www.ipcc.ch/sr15/chapter/spm/> (last visited 2nd August 2019).

Kyoto Protocol to the United Nations Framework Convention on Climate Change, Kyoto, 11th December 1997, 2303 UNTS 162, available at https://unfccc.int/resource/docs/convkp/kpeng.pdf (last visited 2nd August 2019).

Leyla Sahin v Turkey (2007) 44 EHRR 9.

Paris Agreement, Paris, 12th December 2015, available at <https://treaties.un.org/doc/Publication/UNTS/No%20Volume/54113/Part/I-54113-0800000280458f37.pdf> (last visited 2nd August 2019).

Rome Statute of the International Criminal Court, Rome, 17th July 1998, 2187 UNTS 3, available at <https://www.icc-cpi.int/resource-library/Documents/RS-Eng.pdf> (last visited 2nd August 2019).

SAS v France, (2015) 60 EHRR 244.

United Nations Convention on the Law of the Sea ('UNCLOS'), 1833 UNTS 3 (no. 31363).

United Nations Framework Convention on Climate Change ('UNFCCC'), New York, 9th May 1992, 1771 UNTS 107, available at <https://unfccc.int/resource/docs/convkp/conveng.pdf> (last visited 2nd August 2019).

United Nations General Assembly Resolution 70/1, "Transforming our world: the 2030 Agenda for Sustainable Development," UN Doc A/Res/70/1, available at <http://research.un.org/en/docs/ga/quick/regular/70> (last visited 2nd August 2019).

Universal Declaration of Human Rights, United Nations General Assembly Resolution 217A, 10th December 1948, available at <https://www.un.org/en/universal-declaration-human-rights/> (last visited 2nd August 2019).

www.ingramcontent.com/pod-product-compliance
Lightning Source LLC
Chambersburg PA
CBHW022105240926
51848CB00008B/151